WAR MACHINES
AIR

WAR MACHINES
AIR

OCTOPUS
Octopus Books

Introduction

The history of aerial war machines is a far older history than many people imagine. The ancient Chinese used war kites to advantage. Balloons were used for observation purposes in the time of Napoleon. And man's attempts to conquer the air in terms of personal flight date back to the unfortunate Icarus of Greek legend and advance progressively from the great Leonardo's designs for a helicopter to the 'heavier than air' breakthrough achievements of Wilbur and Orville Wright in this century.

In air warfare the milestones of achievement are more readily apparent than in the case of land and sea machines of war. Theory had to wait for scientific know-how. The principles of rocketry have been known, of course, for centuries but only in their sophisticated modern expression can they be said to have become really effective air war machines.

In our times the rush of development has been bewilderingly rapid. But the really important moments stand out—the helicopter, the jet engine, the vertical take-off plane, to name only a few of the more obvious breakthroughs in technique.

The machinery of air warfare demands a sophisticated background technology. More than any other type of war machine an effective air weapon depends on a host of supporting skills and sciences.

This book—like its companion volumes on sea- and land-based machines of war—is in a sense an illustrated catalogue of selected weaponry of the air.

It presents a fascinating picture of technological evolution which helps the reader to build up a 'time-scale' picture in his mind.

Contents

First published in 1975 by Octopus Books Limited 59 Grosvenor Street London W1 under licence from Lynx Press Ltd. 601 Union House Hong Kong

Created and devised by Berkeley Publishers Ltd., 20 Wellington Street London WC2

ISBN 0 7064 0417 3

Distributed in USA by Crescent Books a division of Crown Publishers Inc. 419 Park Avenue South, New York, NY 10016

Printed in Hong Kong

WAR IN THE AIR

THE WAR KITES

The development of the aeroplane, and consequently the great aerial war machine of the 20th Century, was dependent on, among other things, an object we normally regard as a child's toy – the kite. In this chapter we shall look at the kite as an aerial war machine in its own right, and as the necessary precursor to the fighters and bombers that first saw action in the First World War. For we must remember that it was the aerodynamic lessons learnt from kites that enabled the construction of a practicable aeroplane; indeed the first aeroplanes were often nothing more than free-floating, powered kites. This was a principle that Alexander Graham Bell, a keen investigator of the aerodynamic properties of kites (as well as the telephone), saw very clearly: 'A properly constructed flying-machine should be capable of being flown as a kite and, conversely, a properly constructed kite should be capable of use as a flying-machine when driven by its own power.'

First of all, what is a kite and where did it

originate? Clive Hart in his invaluable book, *The Kite*, defines it as a 'heavier-than-air machine held to earth by means of a flexible line and capable of rising to a positive angle with the horizon as a result of the forces created by wind pressure'. The first kites originated in Asia as far back as the 4th or 5th Centuries B.C. In China games were played with them; kite festivals were long held in Korea and Japan; in Melanesia and Polynesia kites were used as aids in fishing. However, they also had a military significance. As early as 196 B.C., one source reports, a Chinese general used kites on a kind of reconnaissance mission. By flying a kite over enemy fortifications he was able to establish the length of the tunnel which would have to be dug in order to get in.

With time, the military use of kites became more sophisticated. By the 6th Century, they were an important strategic weapon, as the following report shows (quoted in J. Needham's *Science and Civilization in China*, published by the Cambridge University Press).

'In the Thai-Ching reign period (547–549) . . . Houching rebelled and besieged Thai-chheng (Nanking), isolating it from loyal forces far and near. Chien Wen . . . and the crown prince . . . decided to use many kites flying in the sky to communicate knowledge of the emergency to army leaders at a distance.'

Dr. Needham interprets this as an account of the use of kites for signalling purposes, with carrier pigeons being used to send out despatches. Kites were similarly used for signalling in 781, when a besieged general sent out messages to fellow-commanders, informing them of his plight. This worked successfully, and the siege was eventually lifted.

We also have an example of kites being used as a propaganda tool. In the 13th Century the Mongols besieged the Chin Tartars in their capital. Chin officers hit on the idea of using kites to drop messages to those of their men who had been taken prisoner by the Mongols, encouraging them to rise up and return to their own side.

Kites in the Far East eventually reached man-carrying proportions. Marco Polo reported the use of man-lifters by fishermen and a Japanese manuscript hints at the use of them in a reconnaissance capacity during a military operation.

The kites used in the Far East were, and still are, greatly varied, depending on their purpose. Animal-shaped kites were used during religious festivals, big rectangular ones with the cord smeared with cut glass or porcelain fought in kite wars, while children happily flew tiny pear-shaped kites with tails. The form of the kite developed considerably over the centuries, resulting in some of the most aerodynamically sound kites ever produced.

The Chinese, for instance, were producing cambered (i.e. curved) wing kites as early as the 10th Century. As we now know, the cambered aerofoil is a lot more efficient than a flat one. A typical Chinese cambered kite would be three feet broad and eleven feet long. A bridle was attached to the centre of one side and a retaining rope on the other. Here again, the Chinese had made important advances, for the use of the bridle greatly increased control of the kite in the fore-and-aft direction. They also experimented with two-cord kites in order to control the kite's angle of attack, depending on the strength of the wind. The frame was usually of bamboo set at a dihedral angle (again insuring greater stability) with the fabric of either silk or paper.

The Japanese 'war kite' could extend up to 15 feet in height and 10 feet across with a harness of seven bridles. It required a strong wind and, unlike the Chinese kite, could not fly without a tail. (Incidentally, a tail is used in flat kites to increase air resistance and thus lift.) The Koreans developed a versatile fighter kite. Rectangular in shape, it was 32 by 28 inches with a bamboo frame and silk covering. A hole was cut in the centre of the fabric about 11 inches in diameter, which enabled the kite to achieve equilibrium in strong winds.

Finally, a word about the Malay kite which was rediscovered by an American, Eddy, in the late 19th Century and used on a number of occasions for aerial photography. The framework consisted of a dorsal spine, slightly curved, across which two horizontal sticks, the same length as the spine, were fitted, one-fifth of the distance along the spine from either end. These sticks were bent, as in a bow, by a piece of cord nine-tenths the length of the spine. Varnished string connected the six points of the kite

Beautifully shaped kites were traditionally flown in China on the ninth day of the ninth month

framework, but the fabric (either cloth or paper) only covered the central rectangular piece. The Eddy kite differed from this in having the total framework covered. The great advantage of the Malay or Eddy kite was that it introduced to the west a stable kite that could fly tailless. It opened the door for further developments in kites; among other things, in their military use.

The Kite Revolution

European kites were probably derived from the Roman *dracones*, dragon-shaped wind-sock standards carried by Roman forces around the 2nd Century A.D. They were quite alarming creatures made by attaching a large, dragon-faced head to the top of a pole. Behind it, billowing in the wind, was a long tube of cloth. These were used for signalling, to identify ranks, but primarily to strike terror into the hearts of the enemy.

The dragon standard continued in use throughout the Middle Ages. At one point it was discovered that it would seem even more frightening if a burning torch was placed in the mouth, thus making the dragon look as if it were belching forth fire and smoke. The Polish historian Drugosz described one such effect:

The kite-carriage was a fanciful idea of 1827

'Among other standards there was, in the Tartar army, an immense banner . . . And at the top of the enemy banner was the representation of a hideous, jet-black head with a bearded chin. During the pursuit on the slopes . . . the standard-bearer began with all his strength to shake the head which was on top of a spear, and from it there poured forth vile-smelling steam, smoke and fumes, which engulfed the whole Polish army. Because of the horrible and intolerable fumes, the Polish warriors, nearly unconscious and half dead, were weak and unable to fight.'

By the end of the 16th Century, however, the popularity of the dragon-shaped kite had dwindled, giving way to the simpler pear- and diamond-shaped designs. At the same time, the military possibilities of the kite were overlooked. It had been relegated to the status of a mere plaything, and it was to be almost 300 years before it was again taken seriously.

Interest is Renewed

The man who paved the way for the kite flying rennaissance was a Bristol schoolteacher by the name of George Pocock. Pocock had the idea of harnessing a large arch-topped kite to a horse-less carriage, and with this contraption he made a successful run along the Bristol-Marlborough road. He also claimed that by means of a similar kite he had actually succeeded in lifting his daughter, Martha, into the air.

The idea of man-lifting kites now began to gain considerable popularity, especially in military circles, where it was quickly realized that they might be very useful for observation purposes. Captain B. F. S. Baden-Powell (the brother of the founder of the Boy Scout movement) was the first European to work seriously on man-lifting kites. In January, 1894, he lifted a man 10 feet off the ground. The kite was hexagonally shaped and 36 feet high. It covered an area of 500 square feet with a sheet of cambric stretched on a bamboo framework. The kite was flown on two lines from which a basket was suspended. With similar kites arranged in tandem he eventually lifted a man 200 feet off the ground. He used the kites for reconnaissance purposes during the Boer War and, with his kites, aided Marconi to set up a wireless service on the battlefield.

The man who really revolutionized kite flying was Lawrence Hargrave, a modest Australian who, in 1893, invented the box-kite. The box-kite was remarkably simple, yet very stable: it had great lifting ability and was almost immediately recognized as far superior to all previous kite configurations.

The kite was made by arranging two cells, or shallow boxes with the bottoms and tops removed, one behind the other. They were held together by variously placed struts and booms, usually diagonal. These were necessary to support the structure but hindered efficiency by adding weight and head resistance. The vertical sides of the box-kite provided lateral stability while the space between the cells provided fore-and-aft stability. Hargrave, himself, was lifted 16 feet by a train of four of these kites arranged in two pairs in tandem.

An American lieutenant, H. D. Wise, using a similar configuration, achieved 50 feet. At the junction of the two lines a pulley was attached with a rope running through it by means of which a 'boatswain's chair', carrying the passenger, was lifted. The main line was wound on a windlass. The kites were made of spruce framework and covered with cotton cloth. The areas of the kites were $22\frac{1}{2}$, 40, 90, and 166 square feet – a total area of $312\frac{1}{2}$ square feet. The main line was a half inch manilla rope.

Lt. Wise also devised a mobile aerial photographic kite kit to be used under battle conditions. It contained eight Eddy folding kites, 6,000 feet of cord, 1 field windlass, rings, pulleys and so on, 1 Wise Universal pointing camera and support, 1 Wise automatic operator for the camera, and 16 regulation signal flags with code staff. Field tests were provisionally successful but Wise's scheme was never implemented.

Cody's Man Lifter

The most successful of all man-lifters were the famous Cody 'War Kites'. Cody was a flamboyant American expatriate living in Britain: a cowboy and showman, and a brilliant and original engineer. For his man-lifters, he adopted the basic structure of the Hargrave box-kite, but he so modified it as to produce, in effect, an entirely new species of kite.

Large wings were built out at the top of the kite, and horn-like structures projected from the sides. These were larger on the front cell and smaller on the back. The wings and, indeed, the entire fabric covering of the cells could be tautened or slackened off as necessary, by means of a special set of controls which also could be

F. S. Cody, on the left, and his famous 'War Kite', taking used to true the kite.

Perhaps more ingenious than the kites themselves was the way Cody assembled them to do the work of man-lifting. He invented a system that resembled the cable-car operations we see up the sides of mountains – only, the top of Cody's cable was fixed to a large kite which hung in the sky. This was the *pilot* kite, and it gave stability and guidance to the entire system. However, it did not provide the main lifting force: this was done by a series of *lifter* kites, usually from two to six, depending on the weather and the weight

part in the first international kite camp on June 25, 1903, on England's South Downs, in Sussex

to be lifted. Each lifter kite took its place at a specific station on the main cable.

Last of all was the *carrier* kite, which had suspended beneath it a passenger basket. When all the other kites were properly positioned the carrier would ascend to the height required. We may note that the aeronaut being lifted could control from his basket the movement of the carrier kite, by means of an elaborate system of lines and pulleys. That is, he could ascend and descend at will; he could also effectively brake when necessary.

With his apparatus Cody could lift a man thousands of feet, and maintain him in the air securely and steadily – an achievement that totally outclassed anything that had ever been accomplished with kites before.

In 1903, the Royal Navy bought four sets of Cody 'War Kites'. The War Office, not to be outdone, in 1905 acquired both the kites and Cody, who was officially installed as 'Chief Kite Instructor' at the Balloon School in Farnborough, later to be known as the Royal Aircraft Establishment.

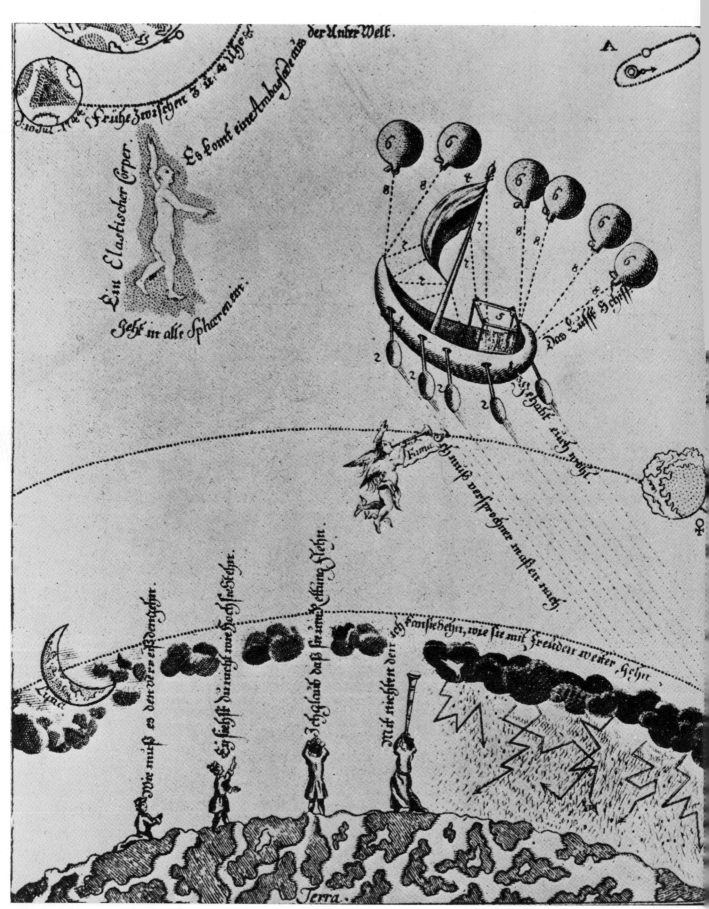

De Lana's impractical flying machine, supported by copper spheres, sets off for another planet, from an engraving of 1744

BALLOONS FOR THE MILITARY

With help of the balloon, man finally succeeded in cutting the cords that bound him to earth. And, with its help, he learned his first lessons in aerial warfare.

A balloon defies gravity because it is lighter than the air it displaces. Roger Bacon, a 13th-Century scholar and scientist, understood this principle and imagined a huge globe, constructed of very thin metal and 'filled with the thin air of the upper atmosphere, or with liquid fire, thus rising into the heavens'. It would take the mass of humanity another six centuries to catch up with this vision.

In the meantime, some four hundred years later, a Jesuit priest, father Francesco de Lana-Terzi, began to take an interest in the latest scientific discoveries. Among them were the findings by Pascal and Toricelli that the atmosphere has a measurable density; also the discovery by Otto van Guericke, that a vacuum can be artificially created.

Inspired by these ideas, de Lana designed a flying machine, which was to be borne aloft by four great copper spheres from which the air had been evacuated. The Jesuit insisted, however, that this design was a theoretical exercise only – which was just as well, since his copper globes would have been instantly crushed by atmospheric pressure had he attempted to put his idea into practice. De Lana had decided that it was safer for man to stay on the ground as God had intended him to. He foresaw with chilling accuracy the possibility of aerial warfare: 'Where is the man who can fail to see that no city would be proof against surprise . . . houses, fortresses and cities could thus be destroyed, with the certainty that the aerial ship could come to no harm, as the missiles could be hurled from a great height'.

If ballooning was ever to be practical, scientists had to discover a substance that was lighter than air. This was achieved in 1776 by Henry Cavendish, who called his discovery 'phlogiston' or 'inflammable air'. The great French scientist Lavoisier, in 1790, named this light and very dangerous gas hydrogen. Meanwhile, in Birmingham, Dr. Joseph Priestley, a chemist and physician, continued the research started by Cavendish and, in 1774, he published his findings in a work entitled *Experiments and Observations on Different Kinds of Air*. With this publication and the increasing pace of enquiry the stage was set for the great era of the balloons.

Henry Cavendish discovered a gas lighter than air
Dr Priestley experimented with 'different kinds of air'

Left: Joseph Priestley, from an engraving published in 1801. Below left: Charles and the Roberts undertake the laborious task of creating sufficient hydrogen to fill their balloon, for the first unmanned hydrogen flight of August 1783. Right: Pilâtre de Rozier and the Marquis d'Arlandres made the first manned balloon flight in a Montgolfièr hot air balloon, on November 21, 1783

The Montgolfièr

Priestley's work aroused considerable scientific interest in Europe. It fired the imagination of Joseph Montgolfièr, a 36-year-old French paper manufacturer. Joseph immediately began to speculate upon the possibilities of hydrogen as a lifting agent and, with this in mind, he carried out a number of experiments. He learned how to produce the gas and with it he attempted to inflate a small paper globe. The attempt was a failure, since the hydrogen passed through the paper like water through a sieve.

Nothing daunted, Joseph changed his line of attack, turning his attention to the possibilities of hot air. He constructed a small silken balloon and lit a fire beneath it. The balloon immediately rose to the ceiling in the most gratifying manner imaginable and Joseph was jubilant. This emotion must have been communicated to his brother, Etienne, who saw the experiment and became a full partner in the pioneer balloon work.

Montgolfièr had no real understanding of the principle behind his hot-air balloon: namely, that air expands when heated and so becomes less dense than the surrounding atmosphere. Instead, he imagined that in the product of combustion – the fumes given off by the fire – he had discovered a new gas. He then spent many months laboriously experimenting with various foul-smelling and unlikely substances, including wet straw, wool, old shoes, decomposed meat and even cow dung – in an effort to find the combination that to his mind produced the lightest form of the gas.

The news of the Montgolfièr balloon spread

across the country like wildfire and in Paris it caused a great sensation among members of the Academy of Science. These learned men, not to be outdone by a provincial paper manufacturer, commissioned one of their members, a physicist named Charles, to build a balloon on their behalf.

Charles was convinced that there was only one gas – hydrogen – which would provide suitable lift for a balloon. Working with two brothers called Robert, who had invented a way of coating silk with rubber so as to make it impervious to hydrogen, and so contain the gas, he constructed the envelope for his balloon.

The Charles balloon, launched in August, 1783, was a great success, and totally outclassed the performance of the Montgolfièr, as the hot-air balloon had come to be called, in terms of the height it attained and the time and distance it travelled. Although the Montgolfièr brothers continued to work on and improve their balloons, it was soon established that the hydrogen balloon was a vastly superior craft. The initial and only advantage of the Montgolfièr was that it could be speedily and easily inflated, in the days when hydrogen generation was a difficult and costly process. However, as techniques for producing and storing hydrogen improved, this advantage was lost.

The first manned balloon ascent took place in November, 1783. The craft used was a large Montgolfièr. Soon afterwards, a manned flight was made in a hydrogen balloon.

Above: Alexandre Charles and Ainée Robert step out of their decorated craft after the first manned flight in a hydrogen-filled balloon. The flight was made from the garden of the Tuileries on December 1, 1783

Right: Charles's first unmanned hydrogen balloon reached almost 3,000 feet above Paris in August, 1783. But when it landed terrified villagers destroyed it with pitchforks, believing that they were being attacked by some strange, shapeless and dreadful monster

Early Military Balloons

As we have seen, the military value of the balloon was quickly appreciated by its inventors. Benjamin Franklin, the American diplomat and writer, also understood its usefulness for 'elevating an Engineer to take a view of an Enemy's Army, Works &c; conveying Intelligence into, or out of, a besieged Town, giving Signals to Distant Places or the like'. He also saw the possibility of large-scale aerial attack:

'Five thousand balloons, capable of raising two men each, could not cost more than Five Ships of the Line; and where is the Prince who can afford so to cover his Country with Troops for its Defense, as that Ten Thousand Men descending from the Clouds might not in many places do an infinite deal of mischief before a Force could be brought together to repel them?'

From theory to practice was a short step. In the wake of the French Revolution, it was suggested that balloons should be used by the French army for observation; and so, in 1794, *L'Entreprenant,* the world's first military balloon, was constructed. This balloon was made especially strong, as it was meant to withstand the wind rather than float freely with it. It was held captive by two cables attached to its equator – the band about its circumference.

L'Entreprenant was manned by a crew of two: one to do the actual observation, and one to handle the controls. Messages were signalled to

Benjamin Franklin foresaw large-scale aerial warfare

the ground with flags, and written reports sent down in small sand-bags attached to the cables.

A demonstration ascent was made for members of the Scientific Commission, who were so impressed by the performance of the balloon that they recommended the formation of the world's first 'air force': the Aerostatic Corps of the Artillery Service. The balloon, together with a company of these *Aerostiers*, was then sent to join the French army at Maubeuge, where it immediately proved its worth in reconnaissance.

From Maubeuge, *L'Entreprenant* and the balloon corps moved on to their greatest triumph, at the battle of Fleurus. This engagement lasted for some ten hours, and during this entire period the balloon – manned by its two observers, Brevet-Captain Coutelle, commander of the balloon corps, and General Morlot of the army – remained aloft. The French army was at all times effectively directed from the air. The result was a resounding French victory, the first ever won on the strength of aerial superiority.

Encouraged by this success, the French built three more military balloons. These were completed in 1796, and each was sent to a different front, together with its own corps of Aerostiers. But, in 1799, Napoleon disbanded the force, for in his own conception of military strategy – a highly mobile *land* force – there was no room for a static object like the balloon.

French military balloons being used as observation posts

American balloon unit inflating a reconnaissance balloon with hydrogen (1862)

The American Civil War

The next serious and large-scale military use of balloons occurred during the Civil War in America. From the beginning, a number of well-known aeronauts had volunteered to do observation work for the Union forces. These early efforts, however, were not successful for a variety of reasons. In the first place, there were problems with the balloons, which were not designed for military use. There were technical difficulties involved in getting the balloons inflated and transporting them in this state to the field. But worst of all was the fact that the aeronauts received very little co-operation or support from the conservative military bureaucracy, which had no experience of ballooning and tended to regard the whole thing as a new-fangled nuisance.

John La Mountain, in 1861, made the first really successful ascent of the Civil War. From a height of 1,400 feet, he spotted two concealed Confederate camps at Fortress Monroe. Later, he used barges on the James River as aircraft carriers, from which he rose 2,000 feet. But his most spectacular achievements were the free flights he made over Confederate territory, relying on a favourable east wind near ground level to carry him across enemy lines, and then discharging ballast and returning with the prevailing westerly currents at higher altitudes. La Mountain repeated this courageous feat not once but many times.

The most important aerial contribution to the Union war effort was made by Thaddeus Lowe. Lowe was an inspired organiser and inventive genius who was eventually befriended by President Lincoln. He was subsequently appointed as a balloonist with General McClellan's Army of the Potomac, and made several captive ascents in his own balloon, the *Enterprise*.

His first major breakthrough was the installation of telegraph equipment in the car of the *Enterprise*, leading the wires down along a cable. On 18 June, 1861, Lowe transmitted his first message to President Lincoln, as follows:

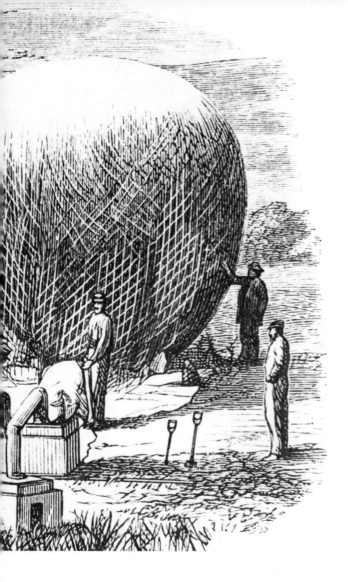

occasion, a balloon was towed for 13 miles, carrying an aeronaut, at 1,000 feet, making continuous observations.

Another important innovation was – finally – the introduction of a 'portable' field generator. These generators were enormous and cumbersome affairs mounted on horse-wagons, but they did serve the purpose for which they were intended. Balloons were no longer exposed to needless risks by being dragged, fully inflated, across the countryside. With the new generators it was possible to fill an average sized balloon in approximately two and a half hours.

The balloons played crucial roles in at least two battles which would otherwise have ended in crushing Union defeats: at Four Oaks and Gaine's Hill. But perhaps their most important contribution was strategic – they hampered enemy movements and made enforced concealment a necessity, so that the Rebel troops had to expend a great deal of energy in avoiding surveillance.

'I have often wondered,' wrote the Confederate General Alexander after the war, 'why the enemy abandoned the use of military balloons early in 1863.'

The reason was the unsympathetic attitude of top army officers. This reached a pitch when General Cyrus B. Comstock was put in charge of balloon operations. Comstock showed so little interest and understanding of the balloonists' efforts that the exasperated Lowe resigned. Deprived of his leadership, the entire balloon corps soon crumbled.

The Confederates made some attempts to utilize balloons, but these were sporadic efforts only. A single Montgolfièr was used for observation by the Confederate General Johnston. However, its practical value was severely limited because it carried no stove and could therefore remain aloft for only a few minutes at a time. It was replaced by a gas-balloon made in Savannah and known as the 'silk-dress' balloon because its envelope was made of bolts of silk of differing colours and patterns. This balloon was captured by Union forces shortly after it was completed.

Undaunted by this set-back, the Rebels built yet another 'silk-dress' balloon. This was flown for almost a year until in July, 1873, it escaped from its moorings in a gust of high wind, and was blown over enemy lines, The Confederates never built another balloon, presumably because by that time the Unionists' balloon operations had been suspended.

'To the President of the United States

'Sir, This point of observation commands an area nearly 50 miles in diameter. The city, with its girdle of encampments, presents a superb scene. I have pleasure in sending you this first despatch ever telegraphed from an aerial station, and in acknowledging indebtedness for your encouragement for the opportunity of demonstrating the availability of the science of aeronautics in the military service of the country, T. D. C. Lowe.'

Lowe went on to design a new military balloon, the *Union* which he also equipped with telegraph apparatus. In this balloon he made many successful observation ascents. He scored another 'first' on September 24, 1861, when, using his telegraph, he directed the artillery to fire on Confederate forces assembled at Falls Church. Never before had aerial technology been used so successfully.

In all, Lowe constructed seven military balloons. He designed an aircraft carrier (a converted coal barge) for use with them and, on one

Above: Preparing a balloon at the Gare du Nord, Paris, to carry dispatches (left) out of the besieged city

The Paris Airlift

We now turn to one of the most spectacular stories of military ballooning history. The scene is Paris, 1870; the Prussians have besieged the city. All surface communications between the capital and the rest of the country have been cut.

During the early stages of the Franco-Prussian war the French government had shown no interest in military balloons. However, the situation in Paris was now desperate, and when a number of aeronauts approached the head of the Post Office, in September, 1870, with a proposal that balloons be used to maintain contact with Gambetta, who was organizing resistance in the provinces, he could not refuse.

On September 23, the professional aeronaut Jules Drurof took off from the Place St. Pierre, with 223 pounds of mail. Some three hours later he landed safely behind enemy lines. It was the start of one of the most astonishing air-lifts in history.

A pigeon-fancier solved the problem of how to get mail back into the city by volunteering the services of his gallant birds. Shortly afterwards, the Parisian photographer Dagron developed special micro-film techniques, which enabled a pigeon to carry film representing 5,000 letters.

Clearly there were not enough balloons or balloonists in the city to sustain the operation for any length of time. And so two great railway stations, the Gare du Nord and the Gare d'Orleans, were transformed into impromptu balloon factories, with hundreds of workers turning out balloons with unprecedented speed. The balloons were large, strong and constructed as cheaply and simply as possible since they were not meant to be used more than once. A number of sailors then in the city were given brief training courses in balloon management. With these fearless men as pilots, the airlift continued.

Naturally enough, the balloons soon attracted the unwelcome attentions of Prussian rifles. These guns were of considerable range and fire power, making it unsafe for balloons at anything less than 3,500 feet. After several narrow escapes, the authorities ruled that in future all ascents would be made by night.

Altogether a total of 66 flights were made, carrying about ten tons of mail, 155 human beings, over 400 pigeons and five dogs. Fifty-eight of these flights were recorded as successful, landing safely in friendly territory. Of the others, two drifted to sea, and a small number had the bad luck to land in enemy territories. The last balloon to leave Paris, on January 28, 1871, carried orders to French shipping to proceed to Dieppe – and news of the French capitulation.

The Paris airlift caused most European powers to sit up and take note. Henceforth, aerial superiority would be of vital importance, and none of the great powers could afford to fall behind. Soon there were balloon schools and balloon corps flourishing in Austria, Germany, France, Russia and England.

British Balloons at War

Captain J. L. B. Templer, a skilled and enthusiastic amateur, was the guiding genius of British military ballooning. Templer's career as a military balloonist started in 1878, when he was granted £150 ($750 at that time) to construct the *Crusader*, Britain's first military balloon. During the course of that career, he developed a balloon corps in Britain that was second to none in the world.

Templer introduced a number of innovations that were essential for effective and practical military operations. For example, the problem of providing gas for balloons in the field had still not been solved to his satisfaction. Templer

Signal arms spread on a British balloon

rejected the 'portable' generators designed by Lowe as being much too cumbersome and slow in action. He finally arrived at a better solution: pressurized steel cylinders in which the gas could be stored until it was required.

Templer also developed a new method for producing hydrogen. The standard procedure for obtaining the gas was through the chemical interaction of zinc and sulphuric acid; this, Templer felt, was unsatisfactory because the gas so generated contained traces of acid which tended to corrode balloon envelopes. Templer therefore evolved an electrolytic process – breaking down water into its component elements – which produced a gas much more free from impurities.

Another outstanding breakthrough was in the construction of the balloons themselves. Previously, all balloon envelopes had been made from fabric – whether silk or simple cambric – which was 'doped' or varnished to prevent any leakage of the hydrogen. As far as Templer was concerned, none of the various varnishes then in use would render cloth sufficiently impervious for his purposes. He therefore started making his balloons from something else – gold beater's skin.

Gold beater's skin is one of the strongest and lightest materials known to man. It is also remarkably impervious. It is made from the lining of the *caecum*, or blind gut, of an ox, each animal supplying only a square foot or so of the

British troops moving an observation balloon in the Transvaal

precious membrane. Because of its expense and relative scarcity, it had hitherto been used only for toys and, significantly, model balloons. Templer and his workers evolved methods for obtaining, cleaning, processing and finally joining many pieces together to form an almost perfect sphere.

By 1899, as a result of these improvements, the British had the most compact and useful military balloon in history. It was remarkably small and economical of hydrogen, without sacrificing any of 'the lift necessary for observation purposes. The war in Africa provided a golden opportunity for the balloon to prove its worth.

The Boer War was fought on several different fronts simultaneously. One consequence of this was that no less than four separate balloon corps each made vital contributions to the British effort. In fact, the scale and influence of balloon operations during this was has never been equalled.

The Second Balloon Section, which was the first to leave Britain for Africa, arrived at Durban, in Natal. From Durban, this section dashed to Ladysmith, where it gave valuable service: locating and observing Boer movements before battle and, during the fight, directing artillery. As it happened, the British lost this battle and Ladysmith was besieged. The Second Balloon Section was trapped – cut off from vital supplies of hydrogen – so, after a month's work,

operations had to be suspended.

However, this was not the end of military ballooning in the area. A balloon section was scraped together outside the besieged town, and this improvised band of irregulars played a decisive role in the battles leading to the lifting of the siege.

One commentator has described these men as 'just about the finest military balloonists that have ever existed'. They kept the Boers under almost constant surveillance, not only following their movements but also seriously undermining their morale.

The Boers retaliated by trying to shoot down the unwelcome observers, but in spite of their unquestionable skill as gunners their efforts were wasted. The balloons proved themselves to be virtually invulnerable. Not only were they very difficult to hit, but they had to be hit many times before they could be brought down.

Two other balloon sections – the First and the Third – also played active roles in the war, in the western area, and their contributions were also invaluable. The balloons continually reported enemy positions and directed artillery during the battle.

It is perhaps ironic that at the point at which balloons reached their highest military development, they were already foredoomed. By the time the war was over, in 1902, the airship had taken their place as the primary aerial weapon.

The French were pioneers of balloon and dirigible flight. Above and below: Aspects of Meusnier's design for a dirigible balloon shaped like a cigar. Another Frenchman, Giffard, actually made an airship powered by steam (right).

SHIPS OF THE AIR

With the advent of balloons, the dream of flight was only partially fulfilled. Balloons could rise, and they could lift useful loads, but they were helplessly at the mercy of the winds.

Almost from the beginning, ambitious aeronauts tried to 'steer' their gasbags through the heavens, by attaching sails or oars or flapping wings to them. Needless to say, these attempts were failures.

But in 1784 (just one year after the first balloon flights by the Montgolfiers and Charles) a Frenchman by the name of Meusnier submitted a design for a dirigible ('directable' or 'steerable') balloon to the French Academy of Sciences. This design called for a cigar-shaped airship, to be driven by three propellers, and it incorporated the revolutionary idea of a *ballonnet*.

Meusnier correctly understood that the spherical shape of the traditional balloon was not suitable for directed flight: that to move forward

through the air, the craft should be elongated or streamlined. He also understood that the airship would maintain this shape only because of constant pressure within the envelope – and if gas were lost, the ship might buckle or crumple in mid-air.

To counteract this tendency – and also as a means of regulating the altitude reached – Meusnier introduced the ballonnet: a small balloon within the main envelope which could be pumped up with pressurized air. As the airship rose and the hydrogen within it expanded, air from the ballonnet would be forced out through a safety valve. Similarly, as the hydrogen contracted (or if it were lost through leakage) air would be pumped into the ballonnet. Such an arrangement, Meusnier pointed out, would also result in the conservation of ballast and of precious hydrogen.

Meusnier's design was unworkable, as he

Santos-Dumont used his No. 9 dirigible to travel above the streets of Paris

himself realized, mainly because of the lack of a suitable power-source. In the years that followed, interest in the idea of dirigibility remained high, but success ultimately depended on the development of an engine which was both light and powerful enough.

During the 1840's, several model airships were built and actually flew, propelled by clockwork or small steam engines. Airship pioneers realized that clockwork could never power a full scale ship. By about 1850, many were seriously investigating the steam engine.

The credit for the first full-sized steerable airship goes to another Frenchman, Henri Giffard. His cumbersome engine, which drove a three-bladed propeller, weighed about 350 pounds and managed to develop 3 horse-power. During its maiden flight – made under almost perfect conditions of no wind – the airship achieved an average speed of 5 miles an hour. It landed safely 17 miles from its starting place.

Giffard himself realized that his machine was seriously underpowered, so much so that, if there had been a wind, the airship would have floated with it just like any other balloon. But a more powerful motor would have meant one that weighed much more, and the craft was already far too heavy.

In 1884, two French Army engineers, Charles Renard and Arthur Krebs completed the construction of their airship, *La France*. This ship was the most advanced and sophisticated to date. Its design was slim and streamlined, coming to a point at either end, and it incorporated such technical refinements as a rudder and elevator, as well as ballonnets. *La France* was powered by an electric motor and developed $8\frac{1}{2}$ horse-power. However, the power-weight ratio was still a piti-

The basket of Woelfert's airship Deutschland, *with the internal combustion engine that drove it*

ful 210 pounds per horse-power because of the weight of the electrical batteries.

The first flight of *La France* was a great triumph. The ship faithfully answered her controls and, successfully defying the winds, made a circular five-mile trip that lasted some 23 minutes – and exhausted the batteries! It was clear that for further progress to be made a still more suitable power source had to be developed.

The answer was not long in coming: the petrol-fuelled internal combustion engine. The first to take this engine aloft was a German named Karl Woelfert, but Woelfert's effort ended in disaster. Hydrogen is an alarmingly combustible gas. Woelfert kept his primitive engine ignited with an open-flame burner. As the ship ascended to 3,000 feet and vented gas – in an instant it was a blazing inferno which fell to earth, killing Woelfert and his engineer, Robert Knabe.

It was left to a wealthy young Brazilian, newly arrived in Paris, to show that the internal combustion engine could indeed successfully power a dirigible balloon. Alberto Santos-Dumont had courage, determination, great mechanical ability and, equally important, plenty of money. He built a series of small pressure airships – each an improvement over the last – whose primary features were their simplicity and lightness. Their design was based, to a large extent, on the work of predecessors making use of, for example, such features as the ballonnet. But Santos' dirigibles were the first to be truly practicable and they turned him, overnight, into the rage of Paris.

His *No. 6* won the Deutsch prize offered for the first flight from St. Cloud, round the Eiffel Tower and back in less than thirty minutes. He used *No. 9,* his smallest ship, as a runabout around Paris – 'dropping in' at his favourite cafés, and

so forth. The Brazilian's exploits, above all, popularized the notion of 'dirigibility' in the French capital.

The next major advance in airship design was the work of the Lebaudy brothers. Their ship, the *Lebaudy I* (nicknamed 'le Jaune' because of its yellow envelope) made its maiden flight in 1902. Strapped to the belly of the craft was an elliptical underframe of steel tubing, which served both to maintain the shape of the airship and as a surface from which to suspend the gondola (or car).

The *Lebaudy I* was therefore, the first semi-rigid airship. It could reach speeds of up to 25 m.p.h., and set several distance records for dirigibles. *Lebaudy I* was damaged in 1903 and rebuilt as *Lebaudy II*. She was eventually acquired by the French army, and became the successful prototype of a series of military airships which served in France and in several other countries.

Left: Santos-Dumont rounding the Eiffel Tower, Paris. Above left: A nasty crash at Saint Cloud. Above right: A cartoon of Santos-Dumont, published in the magazine Vanity Fair, *in November, 1901. Right: The skeleton of the Lebaudy airship, showing the balloon underframe of steel tubing*

Von Zeppelin and the Rigid Airship

The rigid airship owed its existence to two important technological advances made in the 19th Century. The first was, as we have seen, the invention of the internal combustion engine. The second was the discovery of aluminium, the new 'silver made from clay'. This substance, strong yet light, proved to be the ideal building material for the framework of an airship.

The first rigid airship built from aluminium was the brainchild of David Schwarz, a Hungarian engineer. His ship was a total loss. After numerous mechanical difficulties she landed hard and crumpled like an old tin can. Miraculously, her pilot jumped free and did not sustain any injuries.

With the exception of the Lebaudy ships the dirigible had so far shown little practical utility. The small craft of Santos-Dumont and others were not suitable for carrying heavy loads or for making sustained flights. What was needed was something much larger, for experiments had shown that the range and carrying capacity of an airship was in direct proportion to its dimensions. Yet there were limits to the possible size of a ship with a cloth envelope and there was the

Above: Count Zeppelin. Below: David Schwartz's aluminium airship of 1893

constant difficulty of maintaining the lifting bag's smooth contour by internal pressure alone. There was also an ever-present danger that the bag would spring a leak.

The man who found the solution to all these problems was an aristocratic German soldier whose name will always be linked with the rigid craft he pioneered – Count Ferdinand August Adolf von Zeppelin.

According to the tradition of his times, Zeppelin embarked on a career in the army early in life. He was always keenly aware of the military potential of the dirigible, and the launching of *La France* by Renard and Krebs, seriously disturbed him. He was alarmed by the possibility that France might pull ahead in the arms race, leaving Germany lagging far behind. And so he began to work on plans for a rigid airship.

In 1890, after a characteristic clash with Kaiser Wilhelm of Prussia, the hot-headed Zeppelin, now a Lieutenant-General, was asked for his resignation. This meant that the old soldier – he was fifty-two – could henceforth devote himself full-time to his dreams of German aerial superiority.

In 1893, the Count submitted a design for an airship to the German War Ministry, but faults were found with his proposal and it was turned down. Zeppelin remained undaunted and proceeded to work on a second design. This became the prototype for all the future rigid airships – or zeppelins – that came to be built. In 1898 the construction of the ship was commenced.

The basic framework of the dirigible was a skeleton of lightweight aluminium girders, 24 longitudinal beams which connected 16 transverse rings. The interior was thus divided into 17 compartments, each of which was occupied by a hydrogen cell made of rubberized cotton. Each individual cell had an automatic release valve at the bottom, and some had valves at the top which could be operated from the control car. The outer covering was made from impregnated cotton designed to reduce skin friction. The ship measured about 400 feet from bow to stern.

Two open gondolas, connected by a flimsy catwalk, were slung from the bottom of the ship. Each carried a Daimler engine weighing 850 pounds. These engines developed about 15 horsepower, and, for the weight of the ship, it was clear

Zeppelin's giant airship Hindenburg *blazes before crumpling to earth*

that she was underpowered.

The *LZ 1* (Luftschiff Zeppelin 1) made her maiden flight in July, 1902 – a flight which lasted about a quarter of an hour. The ship was very unstable and she barely responded to her controls. She was hauled back to her hangar for repair work but, after just two more flights, she was admitted to be a failure and was broken up.

With determined optimism the Count persisted in his dreams. By 1905, he had got enough financial backing to start work on *LZ 2*. Despite many improvements to its structure, *LZ 2* was doomed to disaster. After her first and only flight she was destroyed by a storm.

Zeppelin doggedly went on to build *LZ 3* which, to the amazement of all concerned, was an unqualified success. The military authorities even went so far as to express an interest in the Count's work, and the army declared that it would purchase an airship if it could make an uninterrupted 24-hour flight. Zeppelin was awarded half a million marks and with this money he constructed *LZ 4*.

LZ 4 made several highly successful flights, but she was jinxed by the bad luck that had plagued Zeppelin's earlier creations. After an attempt at a 24-hour cruise, which was troubled by minor mechanical failures, the ship was

In the night sky, a giant Zeppelin receives a fatal hit

moored in a field for repairs. A sudden thunder-storm struck – there was a burst of flame – and within moments the ship was a charred ruin.

This latest tragedy should have broken the 70-year-old Count's spirit, but by now there was a great deal of public interest in the huge airships. When news of the disaster broke, the German people literally flooded the old warrior with telegrams, letters of sympathy, and most im-portant of all, money – more than six million marks. The German people had decreed that work on the Zeppelins should continue. The Zeppelin factory, therefore, went on turning out airships and the German army acquired *LZ 3* and

LZ 5. By 1911, the navy had also decided to invest in the dirigibles.

Zeppelins in Action

The German people saw the Zeppelins as the 'secret weapon' that would win the war for them. The military authorities had rather less faith. When the war broke out in 1914, the army owned eight airships and the navy, after two losses, just one. The Admiralty therefore embarked on a crash expansion programme.

At the beginning, the army's airships did very

poorly, thus confirming the worst fears of the War Office. They were too heavy, with insufficient lift and low speeds – and were thus horribly vulnerable to ground fire. After two months of battle, four of the eight ships were lost. As a result, their reconnaissance role was abandoned and their operations confined to strategic bombing missions. By late autumn, with the addition of four more ships to the fleet, the army had at its disposal an effective air force that could carry 2,000 pounds of bombs as far as London or Paris. Army Zeppelins made routine attacks on enemy bases, railway yards, and the like. On December 25, 1914, the French towns of Dunkirk, Nancy and Verdun were raided.

By February, 1915, the navy had acquired 10 airships, which they used for scouting and patrol work. The German Admiralty had anticipated that the Royal Navy would establish a close blockade of the North Sea coast, as they had done during the Napoleonic Wars. Instead, a distant blockade was imposed and the German battleships found themselves on the defensive, with all too few vessels available for necessary patrol work. The Zeppelins were drafted to do the job of observing the movements of enemy surface vessels and submarines.

However, the officers of both the army and the navy had dreams of greater things – namely, the bombing of London. They were convinced that if the English capital was raided, the hated Islanders would soon be demoralized and sue for peace. The Kaiser was at first opposed to this plan. He was worried about the 'historic monuments' of London, and he had a tender solicitude for the safety of his 'Royal Cousins', the British King and Queen. Eventually he consented to the bombing of docks and military establishments on the Lower Thames – so long as great pains were taken to spare historic buildings, private property, and 'above all . . . royal palaces'.

The services vied with each other for the honour of conducting the first raid on England. It fell to the Admiralty, which made a totally

The great size of the Zeppelin shows clearly as it hovers above the German fleet at anchor

abortive attempt on January 13, 1915, and another on January 19, in which an insignificant amount of damage was done.

Throughout the late spring and summer the airships of both services attacked Britain. But the raids were not overwhelmingly successful, due mainly to navigational problems – the Zeppelins, flying by night, could not properly find the cities that were supposed to be their targets. Electronic aids, now taken for granted, were of course non-existent; and for better or for worse, most airship commanders had to rely on a 'sixth sense' to get their bearings. Nevertheless, in 1915, 27 of the 47 ships that had set out for England actually made successful attacks.

In the years that followed, the dirigibles made more raids but they did less damage at increasingly higher cost. The aeroplane, in 1914 a primitive craft of limited military value, became more effective and anti-aircraft guns became deadlier and more accurate. The vulnerable Zeppelins were forced to climb higher and higher

The Zeppelin Hindenburg *joins in a Nuremburg rally*

in their efforts to avoid the new British fighters, resulting in a loss of efficiency and a lowering of the load that they could usefully carry.

On September 2, 1916, the German army sustained serious losses in the biggest air-raid on London yet attempted. This marked the end of their offensive use of airships.

The Height Climbers

The Admiralty, however, was not so easily discouraged. It retaliated with the development of 'height climbers', which made their appearance early in 1917.

These 'height climbers', with a capacity of two million cubic feet, could reach the unprecedented ceiling of 20,000 feet. They were the ultimate development of the Zeppelin as a weapon of war. With them, the entire British defence system was at once rendered obsolete. After their introduction the British only managed to shoot down two of the ships before the armistice. However, it must be pointed out that the 'height climbers' brought more problems to the Germans than had been anticipated. They used up enormous quantities of hydrogen (which was becoming increasingly difficult to supply) and their navigation was made more uncertain because they operated mostly above cloud level. At great heights, the speed of the dirigibles was greatly reduced, due to strong gales and currents which were much more frequent than at lower levels. Also, crews suffered horribly from cold and lack of oxygen.

All this, combined with the fact that airships were in constant demand for scouting missions, resulted in raids over London becoming much less frequent, although they were continued until 1918. But they had little more than nuisance value. The dream of bombing Britain into submission was over.

It had been suggested that the navy Zeppelins would have been put to far better use had the Admiralty simply used them as scouts and in conjunction with U-boats, rather than risking them in attack on London. Yet the airships were of some value, if only for the demoralizing effect they had on the British, who dedicated considerable resources and energy to battling the huge marauders.

Nevertheless, by 1918 the lumbering machines were totally discredited as a weapon, even in Germany where no less than 106 had been built. They had failed to win the war.

41

Blimps on Patrol

None of the belligerents of the First World War had put as much faith and resources into the airship as Germany. However, in 1914, most European powers were uneasily aware of the military potential of the machine and felt it their duty at least to attempt to put the airship to work.

Although Britain had experimented with airships from the beginning of the century, she had only a few small vessels in service at the outbreak of war. These were immediately posted to coastal patrol duties. When, early in 1915, threats of German submarines became particularly alarming, the Admiralty ordered the construction of a large number of quick, inexpensive, non-rigid airships for patrol work (type B-limp, soon known as 'the blimp'). Eventually, airship bases were set up all along the British coast, their crews patiently waiting for the tell-tale signs of U-boats.

In 1917, the airships were assigned another job, that of accompanying convoys of merchant ships. The presence of the blimps forced enemy submarines to be on the alert at all times, and also to travel submerged, thus reducing their speed and the length of time they could remain at sea. In short, they played a vital role in the crucial task of keeping Britain's life-lines open. Altogether, nearly 400 blimps were produced in Britain during the years of combat.

France, the United States and Italy also employed airships. In France, where the army possessed about 15 non-rigid dirigibles, early efforts to use them for dropping bombs on enemy targets were plagued by trigger-happy French gunners, who persisted in mistaking them for enemy craft. Eventually, all missions had to be flown by night, since the low ceiling of the ships made them such easy targets.

By 1916, although the French army airships had carried out a fair number of successful raids, it was clear that German anti-aircraft defences were more than a match for them. So the French army suspended operations and handed whatever craft they had left over to the army.

Since the beginning of 1916, the French navy had assembled an airship fleet which they, like the British, were using for coastal patrol duties. Like the British, they found the ships useful for U-boat reconnaissance and eventually assigned them to merchant convoys.

In America, blimps were also used for coastal patrol and actually succeeded in twice sighting

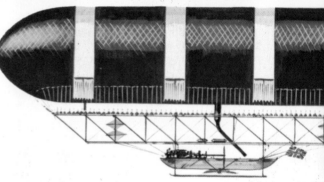

U-boats just outside New York harbour. However, no American airships were ever posted in Europe.

Italy was the only other nation to use airships during the war. Although some of her ships were used for anti-submarine patrols, most were used by the army for bombing and reconnaissance missions across the Austrian lines. These missions were little better than suicidal for they were flown in broad daylight, and the dirigibles were targets for Austrian anti-aircraft gunners. By the end of the war, Italy had lost the majority of her airships and their crews.

A few words should be said about the aftermath of the Great War. Clearly, dirigibles would

U.S.NAVY M

never again be used as primary weapons of combat. However, in America at least, naval authorities had not forgotten the usefulness of the small blimp for reconnaissance and patrol duties. In 1942, and thereafter until the end of World War II, blimps were used, as they had been in the First War, as coastal patrols and convoy escorts. So effective were they that the U.S. authorities claimed that no convoy escorted by a blimp was ever lost to the enemy throughout World War II.

The blimps eventually mastered the procedure of landing on an aircraft carrier, replenishing supplies, and carrying on with their patrols. This came to be a standard practice.

After World War II, United States airship operations were greatly reduced, but the blimps did continue throughout the 1950s and into the 1960s as part of the North American defence chain, employed, as usual, for submarine spotting and as part of the Distant Early Warning radar service, to extend the radar service well out over the Atlantic.

However, by 1962, the American Ballistic Missile Early Warning radar chain was complete. There were no longer any gaps in it for the useful blimp to stop. And so, in 1964, the last airship squadron of the U.S. Navy was decommissioned. Another phase of the air war was over and another machine relegated to the past.

THE INVENTION OF THE AEROPLANE

Leonardo da Vinci has long been recognized as a magnificent artist and a scientist of high achievements. His interest in aviation, however, was discovered only in the late 19th Century. Nevertheless, we now know that this remarkable man produced countless sketches and ideas for flying machines, some of them very complex indeed. Unfortunately, Leonardo, like his less brilliant predecessors, concentrated most of his energy on ornithopters, or flapping-wing designs. To this end, he spent a great deal of time in careful study of the flight of birds. In 1505, he published his observations in the form of a treatise, *Sul Volo degli Ucelli*.

As it turned out, most of Leonardo's notions about the mechanics of birds' flight were fundamentally incorrect. He supposed, for example, that birds supported themselves in the air by a 'downward and backward' motion, akin to a swimming or rowing action. We now know, in fact, that birds are not able to beat their wings in a purely backward motion.

The result was that Leonardo produced a great many designs for flying machines, most of them meant to be borne aloft by human muscle-power. Clearly, however, none of the flapping contraptions would ever have been able to get off the ground.

Experts suppose that Leonardo must have built models of many of his designs and perhaps full-scale versions of one or two. However, it is certain that Leonardo never made any public attempt at flight.

Nevertheless, Leonardo has to his credit a remarkable series of sketches, including several varieties of ornithopters, one of which was even powered by a spring motor. Another was a partial glider, having fixed wings with flapping panels attached to the outer edges. His wing designs, in particular, were elaborate and amazingly life-like.

Leonardo also produced several machines which might be categorized as flying chariots, also certain wing-testing and flight control apparatus.

From our point of view, his most interesting and original inventions were those of the parachute and the helicopter. Leonardo's parachute was a pyramid-shaped affair. Although the design was never practicable, it is nonetheless a true fore-runner of today's parachute, which was 're-invented' some three hundred years later.

His screw helicopter is perhaps the most famous and impressive of his aeronautical designs, meant to rise by means of a helical, or spiral, screw. It was not a workable idea, although there are suggestions that Leonardo may actually have built and flown a model. But this machine owes its greatest importance to the fact that it represents Leonardo's first, and perhaps only, departure from the idea that successful human flight must be based on a detailed imitation of nature. Many historians of flight regret that Leonardo did not pursue this helicopter design, but devoted himself, instead, to his flapping-wing machines. In the end da Vinci's main contribution was to provoke later interest and thought in flying.

The Problems of Flight

Sir George Cayley (1773–1857) was the founder of the modern science of aerodynamics. It was he who first really understood why and how birds fly, and why and how heavier-than-air machines could be made to. He defined the problem of mechanical flight in the following words: 'To make a surface support a given weight by the application of power to the resistance of air.'

Below and right: Leonardo da Vinci's designs for a flying machine were based on the workings of a bird's wing. Pulleys were intended to work the joints.

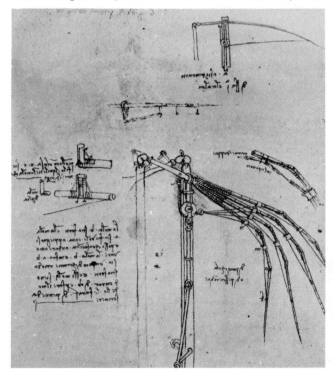

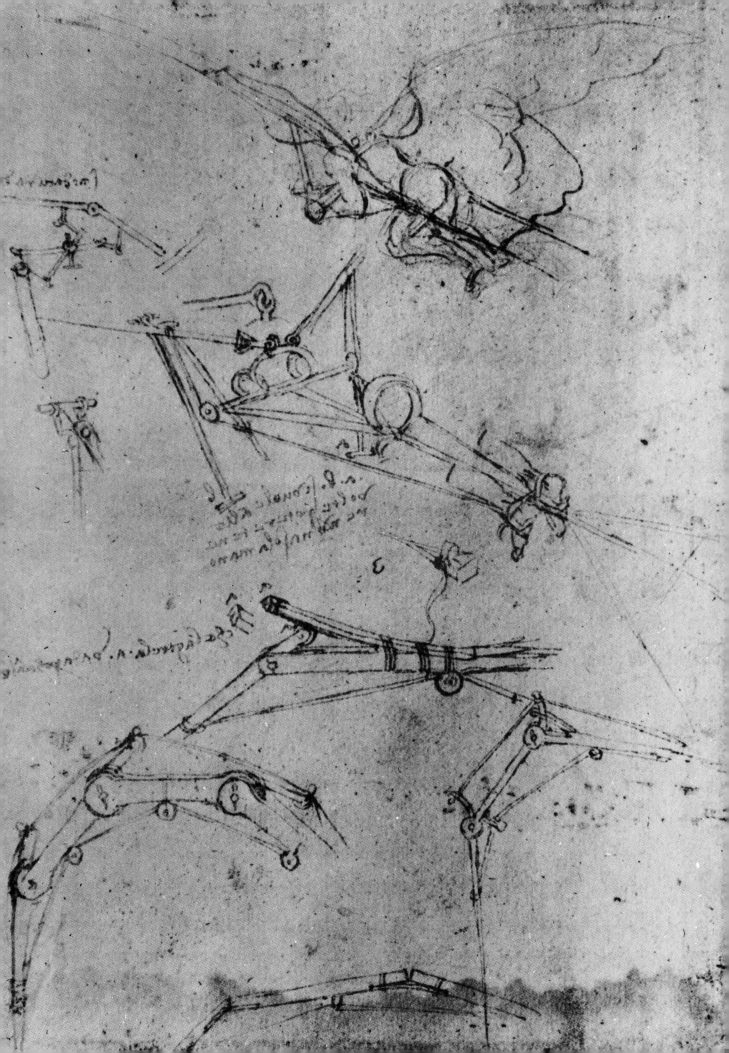

Cayley saw that for the purposes of heavier-than-air flight the forces of *lift* and *propulsion* had to be separated: problems of lift would be solved by the unique properties of the *aerofoil*.

He knew that certain flat-shaped structures, or aerofoils, would support themselves in the air if only they could be made to move fast enough. This principle is appreciated by anyone who has ever skipped stones across the surface of a lake. Cayley understood that *lift* was the result of differential air pressure on the aerofoil. That is, when the aerofoil is travelling through the air, because of its shape a low-pressure area (or partial vacuum) is created on its top surface and, at the same time, a high pressure area is created on the bottom surface. The aerofoil rises, simultaneously 'pushed' and 'sucked' upwards.

Cayley built many gliders and model aeroplanes which successfully illustrated the proper-ties of aerofoils. He soon realized that a *cambered*, or somewhat arched aerofoil would produce the maximum lift.

There is at present in the Science Museum in London a silver disc engraved by Cayley in 1799. On one side of it he illustrated, for the first time, the forces acting on a wing, clearly distinguishing between lift, thrust, and drag. On the other side is Cayley's sketch of a fixed-wing glider, which incorporated such features as a boat-like fuselage and a tail unit with various control surfaces.

Between 1804 and 1853, the Yorkshireman carried our numerous experiments with gliders, and eventually established the basic configuration of the aeroplane as we know it today. His gliders and models featured such innovations as forward main planes, fuselage, adjustable fin and tail planes – in short, they were capable of controlled flight. He also proposed that wings be

superposed, one over the other: thus originating the biplane, triplane etc. Many modern flight historians feel that if an adequate source of power had existed in his time, Cayley might have been the first to achieve powered flight.

The Pioneers

Cayley's work influenced many other thinkers in the world of aviation. In the 1840's, two Englishmen, John Stringfellow and William Henson, designed an 'Aerial Steam Carriage' which incorporated many of the Yorkshireman's basic notions and became the prototype for the monoplane. Later, Stringfellow built a model triplane, which was directly derived from Cayley's work.

From 1850, interest in the idea of heavier-than-air flight gained increasing popularity, especially

Above: William Henson's Aerial Steam Carriage, as it might have appeared in flight. Right: Sir George Cayley.

Langley's steampowered Aerodrome No. 5 flew for more than a minute in May 1895, and landed safely

in France. A French naval officer called Felix du Temple built history's first successful powered model aeroplane, using first clockwork and then steam power. This machine could make short hops and land safely. Many years later he built a full-sized version which also leapt a short distance into the air after a downhill run.

Another Frenchman, Alphonse Pénaud, experimented with aeroplane models, and it is to him that we owe the tradition of powering them with twisted elastic bands. Pénaud also did much to illustrate Cayley's notions on the inherent stability of aircraft.

Clement Ader, an electrical engineer, achieved the distinction of actually leaving level ground in a powered aeroplane. Ader's hop, make in 1890, is not generally considered a real flight, because he had absolutely no control of his craft in the air. His machine, called the *Eole*, was a bat-winged monoplane powered by a steam engine which drove a front-mounted propeller. It had no control surfaces.

Sir Hiram Maxim, the expatriate American who is famous for his invention of the Maxim machine-gun, also took an interest in aviation. Maxim constructed a huge biplane with twin steam-driven propellers, which was to run on rails. The machine was tested, barely lifted itself a few feet clear of the tracks, and came down again, fouling the guard-rails. It was the end of Maxim's work in aviation: an experiment that succeeded in proving very little.

The American S. P. Langley built a number of steampowered models which he called *aerodromes*. These models flew successfully, and Langley was encouraged to build a full-sized machine. However, like many of the men we have discussed in this section, Langley never really studied the problem of control in the air; he concentrated mainly on the question of lift. His full-sized machine was a failure.

Sacrifices Must Be Made

The German Otto Lilienthal was the first to perceive the importance of gaining practical experience in the air. His ultimate goal was

Otto Lilienthal prepares for another dramatic flight

powered flight but he realized that a successful aviator had to be able to control his machine in the air before he gave it the benefit of power. He wrote, in 1896:

'One can get a proper insight into the practice of flying only by actual flying experiments . . . The manner in which we have to meet the irregularities of the wind, when soaring in the air, can only be learnt by being in the air itself . . . The only way which leads us to a quick development in human flight is a systematic and energetic practice in actual flying experiments.'

And so Lilienthal built and tested a number of fixed-wing gliders. He constructed five types of monoplane gliders and two biplane types. His first experiments were made from a springboard near his home, but later he moved his test locations to hills in the surrounding country. Eventually he had his own artificial hill constructed.

Lilienthal's machines were all hang-gliders. That is, he supported himself in them with his arms, leaving his torso and legs dangling free.

He could thus twist and move his body in any desired direction, and so he achieved a measure of control and stability.

His most successful glider was his No. 11 monoplane. He called it his *Normal-Segelapparat* (standard sailing-machine) and in it he could make controlled glides of up to 1,150 feet. He built several replicas of this craft, which he distributed to other aspiring aviators.

In 1895, he began experimenting with methods of flight-control other than body-swinging, and he produced plans for several different control methods. Alas, Lilienthal was never to bring his plans to fruition. In 1896 he crashed on a glide in his No. 11 monoplane. His spine was broken and he died the next day. His last words were reported to be *'Opfer mussen gebracht werden'* ('Sacrifices must be made').

Most authorities are convinced that, had he lived, Lilienthal would have achieved powered flight well before the Wright brothers' triumph of 1903. As it was, Lilienthal directly inspired the Wrights.

The Wrights' Triumph

December 17, 1903, will always remain the greatest date in the history of aviation. For on that date Wilbur and Orville Wright, two bicycle makers from Dayton, Ohio, were the first men ever to achieve powered, sustained, and controlled flight.

The Wright brothers drew much of their early inspiration from the work of Lilienthal. Like Lilienthal, they were determined to gain mastery and control in the air by practising with gliders before committing themselves to powered flight.

In 1899, after having studied all the material on aviation then available, the brothers commenced their experiments. Their first craft was a biplane kite which utilized the technique of wing-warping, or twisting, to achieve lateral (sideways) stability.

The technique proved effective and the

Left: Wilbur Wright at the controls in full flight

brothers used it in their first glider, built in 1900. This No. 1 glider greatly resembled their kite. It was also a biplane, on which the pilot lay prone to reduce head-resistance. The glider was transported to the Kill Devil Hills, south of Kitty Hawk, North Carolina, and the brothers made their first tests.

The results were encouraging and led to the production of a No. 2 glider, but they had many problems with this machine. They guessed that the calculations which they had relied upon (made by Lilienthal and others) were faulty; so they started on a programme of intensive research and study. They even built a wind-tunnel for the testing of wings.

By September, 1902, they had built a fully practical glider, the No. 3. With this craft they made almost a thousand perfectly controlled glides. They were now ready to build their aeroplane.

Since they were unable to find a suitable engine for their machine, the brothers took it upon themselves to design and construct their own: a four cylinder water-cooled motor that developed 12 horsepower. They also did basic research on propellers in order to produce their own highly efficient design.

At last the brothers were ready to test their *Flyer*. On December 14, 1903. Wilbur made the first attempt, but he ploughed into some sand dunes. Three days later, it was Orville's turn: he took off into the wind and flew for 12 seconds, covering about 500 feet in air distance. Three more flights were made on that day – the longest lasted 59 seconds and covered over half a mile in air distance. The aeroplane had finally arrived.

Bleriot's record-breaking aeroplane was the first to fly the English Channel

The Wright Brothers' first flight lasted only 12 seconds. Orville is lying at the controls

In 1904, the Wrights built *Flyer No. II*, and in it they made many brief flights; the longest was about five minutes.

Flyer No. III, 'the first practical powered aeroplane in history' was built in 1905. This machine was fully manoeuvrable: it could bank and turn, perform figures of eight, and remain airborn for over half an hour at a time. The pilot lay prone on it, as was the case with the other Wright Flyers.

An interesting feature of the Wright aircraft was that inherent instability was designed into them, so that the pilot had to 'fly' the machine constantly, righting it after every disturbance, no matter how small, in much the same way that the driver must constantly control his automobile. This policy was eventually seen to be a mistake. European aeroplane designers rejected it, opting for a compromise between inherent stability and sensitivity of controls.

In 1908, Wilbur Wright went to France to demonstrate the brothers' achievements. It is fair to say that this occasion brought about a revolution in the history of European flight.

In Europe, aviation had been more or less moribund since the death of Lilienthal in 1896. When the first garbled reports of the Wrights' work started coming in, a number of Europeans, mostly Frenchmen, were spurred into action. However, none of them grasped the significance of the Wrights' pioneering work with gliders, or the reason for the inherent instability of their machines (i.e. to make constant control necessary). And so, in general, they achieved very little. A few aeroplanes were built but they greatly lacked manoeuvrability, suffering in particular from the lack of lateral controls and from inefficient propellers. It was not until 1907 that any European could stay in the air for even a full minute or begin to describe a tentative circle.

Needless to say, the French were dumbfounded by Wilbur Wright's display of aerial prowess in

Right: Farman flew the first circular kilometre in this plane

1908. The French pioneer, Leon Delagrange spoke for his fellow aviators when he said: *'Eh bien, nous sommes battus! Nous n'existons pas!'* ('Well, we are beaten! We just don't exist.')

The Europeans were at once shamed into a prodigious amount of activity; from 1908, aviation developed rapidly. By the end of 1909, the aeroplane had come of age. This was signified by two events in particular: the historic cross-Channel flight by Louis Bleriot in a frail monoplane he called No. XI, and the great air-show at Reims.

At this airshow, the biplane developed by Henri Farman was particularly prominent. It was a light, rotary-engine powered craft, which used large ailerons instead of wing-warping for lateral control, and achieved an attractive combination of Wright-like manoeuvrability with inherent stability.

Cayley's dream had finally been realized: the era of the aeroplane had begun. Man, at last, had some control over the air.

AIR POWER BECOMES THE CRUCIAL FACTOR

At the outbreak of the First World War, aerial war machines and, specifically, heavier-than-air craft, formed an insignificant part of the armouries of the major world powers. Flying was the realm of a small group of dedicated enthusiasts and was generally frowned upon by the military establishment. Yet within four years air power was well on the way to becoming the crucial factor in warfare – a tremendous upheaval in such a short space of time.

The reason for that upheaval was, simply, the ravenous hunger of total war for any and all sorts of war machines, whatever might obtain that slight but all important advantage over the enemy. Kites, balloons and gliders had all been

Above: A Bristol Box-kite prepares for a flight

German Taube: a monoplane of the First World War

used in warfare, so why not these new-fangled contraptions? Thus it came about that the fragile pre-war aeroplanes underwent an almost magical transformation into sleek and powerful weapons screeching through the skies at unheard of speeds and into heavy, ponderous machines carrying death dealing bombs into the heart of the enemy's territory.

As the war opened the major powers had done little to further the cause of military aviation. The military establishments were conservative in the extreme and refused to acknowledge that the new machines could be of real significance. At best, it was thought, they might serve as extensions of the cavalry scout.

'Aviation is good sport, but for the Army it is useless', declared the French General Foch.

'Experience has shown that a real combat in the air, such as journalists and romancers have described, should be considered a myth. The duty of the aviator is to see, not to fight,' reported the

German General Staff in September, 1914.

'See, Not Fight'

The 'see, not fight' attitude on the part of the authorities resulted in a policy of neither protecting nor arming aircraft. All that was required of the aeroplane was the ability to take off, fly for a reasonable length of time and land safely, specifications that were easily met by the host of aeroplane manufacturers in Great Britain, France and Germany.

The machines used at the outbreak of war were a varied collection culled from civilian manufacturers. Common sights at the front were the various pre-war biplanes like the Maurice Farman M.F.7 'Longhorn', an odd-looking craft with a complicated forward structure. The Bristol Box-kite, so named because of its shape, trained many men to fly. The German Taube, of Austrian design, was a twin-seater monoplane controlled by differential warping of the trailing edges of the wings. Another popular monoplane was the French Morane-Saulnier Type 'L' parasol scout. But whatever the plane, the pilots were confined to a simple observatory role.

In short term policy the authorities were correct. The really important contributions of aircraft to the war effort were in reconnaissance and artillery spotting missions. Thus by spotting

Below: The French Morane-Saulnier, mounting a single gun

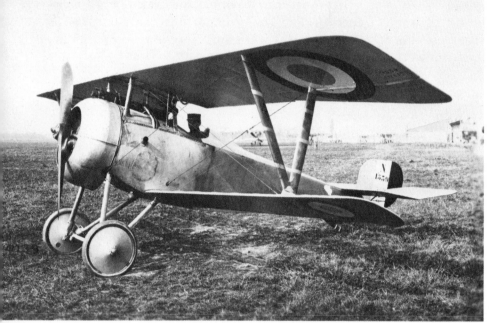

Above left: The Fokker E.III, with interruptor mechanism, was master of the air. Below left: The French Nieuport

Russian troop movements before the Battle of Tannenburg the Germans were able to prepare a victorious counter-offensive. Hindenburg wrote in his memoirs that 'without airmen there would have been no Tannenburg'.

The French showed that they too could use aircraft successfully. On September 3, 1914, French airmen noticed a growing gap between the German First and Second Armies near the Marne. Knowledge of that fatal opening led to the Allied victory in the subsequent battle.

As more and more aircraft took to the skies it was inevitable that pilots and observers should begin to arm themselves with pistols, rifles, hand grenades and even machine guns. The flyers soon found that their impromptu armament was unwieldy and difficult to operate. The demand grew for an aeroplane that could operate as a steady gun platform, and it became rapidly clear that whichever side produced the required warplane would gain the ascendancy in the air.

On the Offensive

Until the development of the ultra-sophisticated radar equipment of the 1950s and 1960s the fighter was basically a flying gun platform. The most efficient means of destroying enemy aircraft was by aiming the plane 'down the barrel'. The problem designers were faced with in 1914–1915 was how to fit a forward firing machine gun in the tractor planes (those with front propellers) of the day.

The first breakthrough came at the beginning of 1915. A French pilot, Roland Garros, asked Raymon Saulnier, the aircraft manufacturer, to fit an interrupter gear into his plane. The idea of the interrupter gear was to stop the machine gun firing when the propeller moved into its line of fire. Saulnier had been working on an interrupter gear for a number of years but had been frustrated by the tendency of machine guns of the day to hang-fire; that is, not to fire at a steady rate.

was also used by British aces with great success. Above: This De Havilland DH2 had a pusher propeller.

Discouraged, Saulnier began experiments along a different line. Instead of trying to interrupt the machine gun fire, why not protect the propeller against damage?

The result was armoured plates attached to the propeller blade to deflect those bullets that would otherwise hit the propeller. The armoured plates were subsequently attached to Garros' Moran-Saulnier airscrew. The result was phenomenal. Within two weeks Garros had shot down five enemy aircraft, an incredible achievement in those days. The deflector plates had made the aeroplane a powerful *fighting* weapon. The offensive capabilities of the aeroplane could no longer be doubted. A war machine was born, and with it the great aerial arms race.

Interruptor Gear

The deflector plates had proved a point but also became a dead-end line with no potential for de-

velopment. It was an interim mechanism only in use until the real thing could be perfected. And the real thing was the interrupter gear.

On April 19, 1915, Garros was shot down behind enemy lines and, before he could destroy his plane, the Germans had seized it. The very next day the armoured airscrew was being studied in Anthony Fokker's workshop. Within a few months the Fokker team had come up with a prototype fighter (then known as a scout) embodying a new Parabellum machine gun firing forward through the airscrew by means of an interrupter mechanism. By the middle of the summer 11 German pilots were supplied with the new fighter, the Fokker Eindekker 1.

The Fokker Scourge

The effect of Fokker's invention can best be gauged by the epithet given to those winter months of 1915–1916, when Fokker Eindekkers I,

57

II and III reigned supreme – the Fokker scourge. The Germans were hitting back and with a vengeance. For nine months the Fokker gave the Germans undisputed mastery of the air and it was not until the spring of 1916 that the legend of Fokker invincibility began to crumble under the impact of a second generation of improved Allied war planes.

Until the Fokker appeared over the skies of Europe pilots believed that they were invulnerable to enemy aircraft bearing directly down on them. It was inconceivable that fire power should come through the propeller. Surprise was therefore a major factor in the success of the Fokkers, but as aeroplanes they had their disadvantages. They were structurally mediocre. The E.1. was underpowered by its 100 horse-power Oberursel engine; the bracings on the single wing were vulnerable to hostile fire and the wing itself could not stand up to excessive strain.

The Allies Hit Back

The Fokker scourge was eventually stemmed by the introduction of a better class of machine. The British sent in their two-seater Vickers Gun Bus and the single seater pusher DH2. The rear-mounted engine on the DH2 gave a clear forward field of fire for the Lewis gun, which, because it did not shoot through the propeller, had an unrestricted rate of fire.

The French adapted their Nieuport Bébé and came up with the Nieuport 17, armed with a synchronized Vickers gun in addition to the Lewis mounted on the top plane and operated by a Bowden cable. The Nieuports were favourites with the British aces and Albert Ball and James McCudden scored some of their most impressive kills in the French machines.

The first British forward-firing fighter was the graceful two-seater Sopwith 1½ Strutter. The 1½ Strutter was fitted with a Vickers machine gun linked to a Ross interrupter gear. The observer was equipped with a Lewis gun. The 1½ Strutter was undoubtedly the best fighter/reconnaissance plane of its time. Development, however, moved at a rapid pace in wartime and the Strutter was soon outclassed by the German Albatros D series of fighters.

The Albatros Outguns All

The old pusher style DH2, the Nieuports and the

Sopwith 1½ Strutter gave the Allies the necessary fighting power to wrest control of the skies from the Germans. But the Allied supremacy was very short-lived for the Germans had been experimenting with a new series of fighting machines: the Albatros D.

The Albatros D series produced some of the finest fighter planes of the war. The biplane structure was fitted with a powerful 160 horse-

Planes of the First World War. Top: Fokker D-VII. Right: Pfalz D-XII. Bottom: Nieuport 28

power water-cooled Mercedes engine (in later marks, the Albatros D reached 118 miles an hour). In addition to its fine flying capabilities the Albatros had formidable fire power in its twin forward-firing Spandau machine guns. As a result the biplane had the highest firing rate (1,000 rounds per minute as opposed to 300 for the Sopwith 1½ Strutter) of any warplane then available. In sum, the Albatros D could out-manoeuvre, outfly and outgun any comparable machine.

Hunting Squadrons

A weapon in itself does not make a great war machine; its proper use does. Fighter efficiency was increased by forming the fighters into *Jagdstaffeln* (*Jastas* for short) hunting squadrons.

German fighter ace, Max Immelmann

Fighting techniques developed by the great German aces, Max Immelmann and Oswald Boelcke, during the Fokker scourge, were refined and applied to formation fighting. The Jastas became the most lethal aerial war machines of their day. Unconstrained by the escort and observation duties which were expected of their opposite numbers, the Jastas roamed the skies with one mission–to seek and destroy enemy aircraft.

The Red Baron Strikes

The squadron leader of Jasta 11 was a young (23), arrogant Prussian officer, with ten kills to his credit and a growing reputation when, in 1916, he met his toughest challenge–Major Lanoe G. Hawker, British ace and holder of the Victoria Cross. The Prussian was Manfred von Richthofen,

later to become famous as the Red Knight or Baron, the greatest ace of the First World War.

Hawker, flying a DH2, had been instrumental in stemming the Fokker onslaught of 1915–1916. But the DH2 was totally outclassed by late 1916, when the skies began to fill with the sleek and vicious Albatros, with their deadly twin Spandaus. Hawker had been cornered a number of times by German pilots and it was only due to his amazing skill that he escaped. Twice he was shot down, once wounded. Yet he continued to go out on patrols with the 24th Squadron.

On November 23, 1916, Hawker ran into a German scout. The scout was an Albatros but Hawker had the advantage of height. He pointed the nose of his DH2 downwards and threw it into a dive, hoping to catch the German from behind (the fatal blind spot). At 10,000 feet Hawker eased out of the dive, passing the Albatros with guns blazing. He failed to destroy the plane and lost his sole advantage.

From then on the DH2 and the Albatros looped round and round, each trying to get behind the other. But the Albatros was the superior machine. It could turn tighter and fly faster than its opponent. The hunter now became the hunted. The best that Hawker could hope for was a small slip on the part of the German that would let him escape. But Richthofen was too clever. This was to be a duel to the finish.

'Round and round we go in circles, like two madmen, playing ring-around-a-rosie almost two miles above the earth,' wrote Richthofen in his

The Albatros D.VA. The Albatros D series completely outclassed Allied machines

combat report. For twenty minutes the two parried and counter-parried but, in the end, the better machine told. 'My machine,' continued Richthofen, 'gave me an advantage by being able to climb better and faster. This enabled me at last to break the circle and manoeuvre into a position behind and above him.' By this time the two had lost so much height that they were skimming the tops of trees and farmhouses.

In a last endeavour to foil his enemy, Hawker gave full reign to the left rudder in an attempt to meet Richthofen head on. The attempt failed. At fifty yards the German opened fire, splattering bullets across the fuselage of the DH2. One bullet hit home, smashing through Hawker's skull. The pilotless craft plunged earthwards. Richthofen remarked that Hawker was a 'brave man, a sportsman and a fighter' but, against a superior war machine, Hawker was helpless.

It was incredible he managed to survive as long as he did. His fellow pilots did not fare so well – their average life expectancy was 11 days.

The Albatros scourge was far, far worse than anything experienced previously. It culminated in the Bloody April of 1917. Then the Allies began to produce machines that could match the Germans. Among these was the Sopwith Camel.

The Sopwith Camel

The biplane Camel was built around an air-cooled rotary engine (130 horsepower Clerget). It called for a great deal of skill in handling.

The Camel, built to challenge the German Albatros

Armed with twin Vickers guns mounted in the fuselage, the Camel had both firepower and manoeuvrability. It could climb to 10,000 feet in 10·5 minutes and maintained a maximum speed at that height of 112·5 miles an hour. The Camel was the classic rotary engine fighter of the war.

The War's Top Fighter

The Camel, the SE 5 and the SE 5A, the Spad XIII were the machines that put an end to the Albatros supremacy. The war, however, was not over and, twice before, the Germans had proved that they could wrest control of the skies from the Allies with superior war machines. In late 1917 and early 1918 they made one last stab at producing the ultimate fighter aeroplane. Draft specifications were submitted and trials held.

The new Fokker biplane completely out-performed all its rivals. A single-seater with a slim fuselage built around a 160 horsepower Mercedes engine, it was able to fly at 118 miles an hour and climb to 10,000 feet in 9·5 minutes. Its most amazing asset, however, was its uncanny ability to hang on its propeller and fire straight upwards, a manoeuvre that caused Allied planes to stall. The Fokker D VII was certainly the war's best fighter but came too late to revive the failing fortunes of the German Air Force.

Overleaf: A bombing formation of British D.H.4s close up to beat off a fierce attack of biplanes and Fokker triplanes with concentrated machine gun fire. A painting by G. H. Davies

The Flying Circus

As the war dragged on, the lonely ace scouring the skies for an unsuspecting enemy gave way to large fighter formations. The Germans had taken the lead with the establishment of Jastas but the British, Americans and French soon followed suit. The French took particular pride in their *Escadrille de Chasse* (Hunting Squadrons) and chief among these were the élite squadrons of *Les Cigognes* and *Les Sportifs*.

The Germans responded by regrouping their Jastas into larger formations known as *Jagdgeschwader*. The Geschwaders were sent in at critical points on the front and moved up and down the lines of their own transport units. Their garishly painted aeroplanes (leading the Allies to dub them 'flying circuses') presented a formidable aspect in the air. And for a time they gained local tactical superiority. But the overwhelming Allied numbers, their increasingly efficient organisation and the improved quality of the Allied machines left no doubt as to the final outcome.

The Germans lost the war but not for lack of superior aerial war machines. In technological and tactical development the Germans were far ahead of the Allies. It was the Germans who discovered that the true aerial war machine was a combination of plane and tightly formed unit and, with their war machines, they won astounding air victories. It is instructive to look at the casualty figures for the war: the German Air Force lost 5,853 men killed, 7,302 wounded and 2,751 missing and taken prisoner as well as 3,128 aeroplanes. The British Air Force alone lost 6,166 men killed, 7,245 wounded and 3,212 missing and taken prisoner.

Air Power and Bombs

Even while fighters and fighter tactics showed an increasing sophistication, important developments were taking place in other areas of aerial warfare. It must be remembered that fighters were produced in the first place to provide protection for reconnaissance and bomber aircraft. We have already noted the effects and early successes of reconnaissance missions. The future of air power lay, however, in the concept of strategic bombing.

Almost from the beginning of man's dream of flight, he had envisaged the hostile purposes to which aeroplanes could be put. It needed little imagination to realize the destructive potential of missiles hurled from high places. Once warfare

developed beyond the primitive hand-to-hand fighting, missiles of one form or another, from arrows to the latest in military cannon, dominated the battlefield.

The idea of dropping bombs on the enemy from aircraft was, in many ways, an extension of artillery bombardment. But there was one crucial difference – the bomber could penetrate far behind enemy lines, the so-called 'third dimension'. It was on this crucial difference that military thinkers after the First World War

Far left: Igor Sikorsky was a pioneer in three different aeronautical fields: multi-engined aircraft, trans-oceanic flying boats and helicopters.
Below: Sikorsky's four-engined Ilya Mourometz was used for bombing raids.
Left: The Italian Caproni Ca series proved useful bombers. This is a Ca3.

developed the concept of strategic bombing, an idea that was, eventually, to have a tremendous influence in the creation of massive bombing war machines. But we are getting ahead of our story. In 1914, the real problem was a technological one, for the effective bomber aircraft did not exist.

Gavotti's Raid

Even before the war there were precedents for bombing raids. An Italian, Lt. Gavotti, an observer in the aeroplane, dropped four bombs on enemy targets (Turkish) in the Libyan war of 1911. The bombs were Swedish grenades adapted for aerial use. They caused a limited amount of damage and a great deal of consternation; it was a severe shock to discover the enemy attacking well behind the front lines.

Despite Gavotti's example the introduction of an aircraft specifically built as a bomber had to wait upon the war, which gave the necessary impetus to the development of that machine. By 1918, mammoth four engine machines were capable of carrying substantial payloads over considerable distances.

The Bomber

The first moves towards the true bomber were made in Russia, when Igor Sikorsky constructed the first four-engined aeroplane, the *Ilya Mourometz*. The *Mourometz* was sent on bombing raids against Poland in 1915, but internal crises prevented further innovations.

The Italians developed a highly successful bomber in 1915, the Caproni Ca series. The Ca 1 was a biplane with a wing span of nearly 73 feet. Powered by a 100 horse-power Fiat water-cooled engine it attained a maximum speed of 72 miles an hour, had a ceiling of 13,100 feet, and carried a 1,000 pound payload. A central nacelle held the crew of two pilots and one observer/bombardier/gunner. The Capronis were used in tactical air raids on Austrian positions in the Adriatic. One raid, on February 18, 1916, dropped four tons of bombs on Ljubljana.

The Germans turned to bombing raids early, with the use of the Zeppelin airship. The Zeppelin, however, proved much too vulnerable as a military craft, so the Germans, working furiously to find an effective replacement, came up with the Gotha.

The Gotha was a twin-engined pusher biplane with a wing span of about 77 feet. It operated at a

Left: The Gotha, a formidable bomber.
Below: The Handley Page 0/400, with wings folded for transport, and in flight

The Handley Page V/1500 super-bomber; too late to bomb Berlin

ceiling of 15,000 feet, putting it out of reach of most fighters, and it carried a load of up to six 112-pound bombs for raids on England.

The Gotha was closely followed by the Giant, a larger and faster aeroplane. This had a maximum speed of 84 miles an hour, a ceiling of 14,170 feet, and endurance of up to 10 hours.

The Gotha and Giant raids on England were carried out from May, 1917, through to May, 1918, causing extensive damage. As weapons the Gothas and Giants were formidable, but they were not employed in sufficient concentrations to have a serious effect on the course of the war.

However, to a public unused to this kind of aerial warfare, the bombing raids were terrifying. A public outcry resulted in two very important decisions. The first, on the recommendations of the Smuts committee, led to the establishment of the Royal Air Force, as a separate military service, on April 1, 1918. The second decision was stimulated by the cry for revenge – the construction of heavy bombers to raid Germany and pay the Germans back.

The British had already been experimenting with heavy bombers. In 1916 Frederick Handley Page was told to build a 'bloody paralyser', and he did – the Handley Page 0/100. With a wing span of 100 feet, it was the largest plane to go into action on the British side. It was powered by the new Rolls-Royce Eagle Mk II engines which gave it a speed of 85 miles an hour at 7,000 feet and a range of 700 miles. The 0/100 weighed 14,000 pounds fully laden and carried up to 16 112-pound bombs. It proved itself an effective tactical bomber in attacks on railway junctions and the Saar Steel works.

By the end of the war the British had constructed three new super-bombers – the Handley Page V/1500. The 126 feet wide V/1500s were powered by four Rolls-Royce 375 horse-power

Eagle engines and reached a maximum speed of 97 miles an hour at 8,750 feet. They could carry up to 7,500 pounds of bombs, and stay in the air for 14 hours. They were the biggest and best the war had produced, and were all set to carry out bombing raids on Berlin when the war ended.

Though they began in 1915, bombing raids did not become really effective until late in the war. In the early years both sides were groping for the most effective means of deploying bombers. It was only through the experience of war that the policy of formation flying and concentrated bombing on strategic targets was formulated. Once these aims were realized the bomber force became a powerful machine of war. But by that time the war was near its end. The real fruits of strategic bombing would only be reaped in the Second World War.

The war had seen a tremendous development in military aircraft. The motley collection of 1914

planes had become, by 1918, highly specialized war machines. Fighters carried twin machine guns firing at a rate of 1,000 rounds a minute, whereas at the beginning of the war aeroplanes went unarmed. Reconnaissance craft were flying almost twice as fast as their 1914 precursors, and a completely new class of plane had arrived on the scene – the heavy bomber. By the end of the war the large bombers, with a tail as big as single seater fighters, were carrying bomb loads of up to four tons to enemy targets 800 miles away.

Beyond the immediate innovations lay the massive experience gained by manufacturers and pilots in building and handling aircraft. Experiments were carried out on various forms of planes, from semi-monocoque monoplanes to the extremely manoeuvrable triplane. It was this experience which laid the foundation for the revolutionary developments of the inter-war years.

ADDING STRENGTH AND SPEED

The inter-war years was an heroic age in aviation history. From the sport of the wealthy, aviation became a multi-billion pound industry. In those years the great airliners were established and the great aviator-explorers set their mark on the world. The names of Alcock and Brown, Charles Lindbergh, Richard Byrd, Amelia Earhart and Charles Kingsford Smith became household words, fearless aviators who blazed pioneering trails across the skies. A host of technical innovations made aircraft bigger, faster and safer.

In the military field, the inter-war years were important for the work of Trenchard in Britain, Colonel 'Billy' Mitchell in the United States, and Brigadier-General Giulio Douhet in Italy. To the point of sacrificing their careers, they advocated the importance of air power in any future war – specifically, long range strategic bombing.

Trenchard was more concerned with the preservation of an independent air force in the face of pressure for its return to army control. Douhet and, to a lesser extent, Mitchell, were responsible for the concept of the self-defending bomber. They assumed that such a bomber could effectively break through all opposition and reach its target, thus gaining advantage in the war. Their ideas led to the development of the long range, self-defending strategic bombers: Blenheims and Wellingtons in Britain, and the B-17, B-24 and B-29 in the United States.

The ideas of strategic bombing were beginning to be formulated even during the First World War. The problem at that time was that the technical requirements to carry out such a policy did not exist. The great developments in aircraft design over the next 20 years made possible what was previously only a dream.

Streamlining the Fighter

Much of the impetus of post-war design was towards streamlining. Practical experiments and scientific theory made the aviation world aware of the extreme importance of streamlining for improved performance.

As early as 1894, the English theorist, F. W. Lanchester, had shown scientifically that the drag of a perfectly streamlined aeroplane was no more than that caused by the friction of the air moving over its surface plus the drag necessary to sustain it in the air. The German aerodynamicist, Ludwig Prandtl, arrived at similar conclusions independently. However, the significance of the Lanchester-Prandtl theory was not fully realized until after the First World War, chiefly due to the lack of suitable aeroplane material. Advances in metallurgy and the perfection of the *cantilever* monoplane (with the wings attached to fuselage without any external support or bracing) went a long way towards fulfilling the vision of the fully streamlined aeroplane.

The Fokker D-VII; once Germany's most famous fighter

The first tentative steps in that direction were made by the Germans. Their most famous fighter of the war, the Fokker D VII, incorporated thick-section cantilever wings. Earlier, in 1915, Junkers designed an all-steel cantilever monoplane. It did not fly well because the steel skin carried all the stresses, which it was not built to do. Platz, the Fokker designer, used plywood, which at that time was more suitable as it was inherently lighter. The Junkers monoplane had low set wings at a pronounced dihedral angle, while the Fokker monoplane wings were laid horizontally across the top of the fuselage. The introduction of retractable undercarriages, another forward step in the streamlining process, proved the Junkers design more efficient, for it allowed a shorter and lighter undercarriage.

Stressed Skin for Strength

The problem that Junker faced in the construction of his monoplane – inordinate stress on the

Boeing 247, made more efficient by the variable pitch propeller

steel skin – was resolved by another German, Dr Adolph Rohrbach. Over a 10 year period Dr. Rohrbach experimented with and perfected a new mode of aircraft construction, the stressed-skin method. Rohrbach's revolutionary concept was to have the skin of the aeroplane carry the primary structural loads. He achieved the desired result by building his wing around a central box section girder of thick duralumin sheet.

Rohrbach's work was extended by a colleague, Dr. H. Wagner. Dr. Wagner discovered that sheet metal could carry an increased load after it had buckled. Until Wagner formulated his theory designers automatically assumed that their designs were a failure if the sheet metal buckled. A lot of effort and money was expended to avoid this 'fault'. Wagner's theory of the diagonal-tension field team formed the basis for aeroplane structures from the mid-1930s. Basically, the theory postulated that sheet metal skin carried its greatest stresses diagonally, and if it were supported by stiffeners around the edges the skin would increase its loading capacity after buckling. In fact, tests showed that buckled skin carried up to 85 per cent greater load.

By the mid-1930s the all-metal, stressed-skin, cantilever monoplane began to replace the wood and fabric planes with their complex systems of struts and braces. The new type of plane displayed a greater efficiency and had a longer life than the conventional aircraft of the period. An American governmental report on 'Those new types of machine' stated that 'because of their structural permanency, their high load carrying capacity, and their maximum speed, they will undoubtedly be the airplanes of the future'. Not only did they become the new aeroplanes of the future, but also the new war machines of the future.

Engine Cowling Reduces Drag

Streamlining took another major step forward with the invention of engine cowlings. One of the great problems with the air-cooled radial engine, which in the inter-war years began to replace the rotary engine, was that it produced an enormous drag on the aeroplane. Efforts to reduce the drag were complicated by fears that enclosing the engine would hinder its cooling. Rotary engines had been cowled but because, with the rotary, the engine itself moved in a circular motion, cooling was not a major problem.

In England, H. L. Townsend of the British National Physical Laboratory found that a ring mounted round a radial engine reduced drag. In the United States, the National Advisory Committee for Aeronautics conducted tests which showed that a complete cowling system reduced drag far more effectively than the Townsend ring, without, in any way, hindering engine cooling. The NACA cowling was quickly adopted by various commercial airliners, which proved its value by increasing their performance and reducing their operating costs.

The introduction of slotted flaps and the variable pitch propeller were two further funda-

Handley Page 32 Hamlet, with wing flaps

mental innovations which helped transform aeroplanes into the efficient transport and military machines that they became.

As its name implies, the variable pitch propeller is one where the pitch (the blade angle with respect to airflow) of each blade can be varied. The propeller could thus adapt itself to changing airflow conditions enabling it to make full use of engine power.

The first practical variable pitch propeller to go into regular operation, the Hamilton-Standard, was invented by F. W. Caldwell in 1930. He used a hydraulically operated system to change the pitch of the drop-forged aluminium blades. Installed in the Boeing 247 in 1933 the variable-pitch propeller reduced normal take-off run by 20 per cent, increased the aeroplane's rate of climb by 22 per cent and doubled its maximum altitude on one engine from 2,000 to 4,000 feet, a successful demonstration of the aerodynamic properties of the variable-pitch propeller.

The Caldwell system was followed by the Turnbull propeller which used an electric motor to operate the propeller. During the Second World War production of the Turnbull propeller became so great that, for a while, the United States government refused to pay royalties, considering the payments excessive.

Soon afterwards the invention of the constant speed propeller enabled the pilot to maintain a constant engine speed under any flying conditions. This was effected by automatic changes of propeller pitch.

Slots and Flaps

The aerodynamic properties of wing flaps and slotted wings had been known before they were put into general use. As with the variable pitch propeller they were only suitable for monoplanes, and thus had to wait for the development of the cantilever monoplane.

The lifting power of the slotted wing was first discovered by a young German pilot, G. V. Lachmann. While recovering from an air crash Lachmann pondered on the problem of the stall (the point at which the lifting power of air is inadequate to support the aeroplane). Since a stall always occurs when the aircraft is operating at a high angle of incidence (the angle at which the wing hits the airflow), Lachmann reasoned that, by slotting the wing, each section would act as a separate wing operating at a normal angle of incidence. After much difficulty he convinced Prandtl to test his theory. The tests were a great success. Lift on slotted wings was increased by 63 per cent.

At the same time Handley Page, working from wind tunnel tests, had discovered the impact of the slotted wing. Lachmann joined the Handley Page organization and soon they had developed the multi-retractable slats which increased lift by more than 300 per cent – an enormous advance in aeroplane design.

The slotted flap followed on naturally from the slotted wing. In its simplest form the flap is a hinged section of the trailing edge of the wing.

When hinged downward there was a notable increase in lift (useful for take-off and in near-stall conditions) and drag (useful for landing). The efficiency of the flap was increased by adding a slot at its leading edge where it connects with the major portion of the wing.

The combination of slotted wings and flaps was an enormous advance in aeroplane design, and increased speed and wing loading on aircraft. Fighters were the planes that benefited most from the invention of the flap for they were more prone to stalling in the extreme conditions in which they were flown.

Other developments which were of great importance but not directly connected with aeroplane design were the invention and refinement of navigational aids such as the horizontal gyro, which indicated the pitching and banking movements of the aircraft, and the directional gyro, which indicated the heading of the aircraft. These blind flying instruments released the pilot from having to make reference to landmarks, an especial advantage under the rigours of wartime flying.

One of the Great Warplanes

One aeroplane which incorporated many of the new design features enumerated above was the

DC-3 (also known as the *Dakota* and C-47). The DC-3 has been called the finest aircraft ever built. When production ceased in 1945 some 13,000 aircraft of this model had been completed. It served as a commercial transport aeroplane and, during the Second World War, was one of America's finest troop transport machines.

The DC-3 was powered by two Cyclone engines (1,000 and 1,200 horse-power) and the wings were constructed on Northrop's multi-cellular design. It was an extremely durable aeroplane and displayed amazing performances during the war. It could continue to fly even after huge chunks of wing had been shot off or when riddled with holes. The DC-3 was, undoubtedly, one of the great warplanes. The basis for that greatness lay in the revolutionary changes in aircraft design in the 1920s and 1930s.

As the 1930s drew to a close it seemed more and more likely that, once again, the world would be at war. The great powers turned their attention to developing military aircraft which would give them the advantage. The dominance of air power in the Second World War rested completely on the great developments of the previous 20 years. Without them there would have been no aerial war machines.

Below: The sturdy Douglas C-47

FIGHTERS OF THE SECOND WORLD WAR

In his *History of Warfare* General Montgomery wrote: 'When I myself rose to high command in 1942, I laid it down as an axiom that you must win air battles before embarking on the land or sea battle'. Military thought had come a long way from the early days of the First World War when Foch had declared aviation good sport, but useless in war. It was now, going to the other extreme, acclaimed as the single most important factor in warfare. The reason for the aeroplane's great importance as a war machine was the revolutionary developments in aircraft design discussed in the previous chapter. On the basis of that revolution were built the great aerial fighting machines of the Second World War.

As with the First World War the demands of wartime led to rapid escalations in fighter efficiency and power. Both the Allies and the Axis powers were involved in a deadly arms race searching for the big breakthrough that would give mastery of the air. That breakthrough did come, but not till the end of the war. The introduction of jet aircraft would have given, with time, air superiority to the Germans. Fortunately, that potentiality was underestimated by Hitler. In the meantime, the piston-engined aircraft was extended to its very limits.

The Top Fighters

At the outbreak of war the twin-engined fighter-bomber was thought to be effective. But, gradually, the comparatively slow speeds of these machines led them to be withdrawn to the role of night fighter. Very quickly the single engined monoplane became the most effective machine: Spitfire, Hurricane, Me-109, Fw 190 and the P-47 Thunderbolt are examples of these.

One drawback found by the Germans during the Battle of Britain, and by the Allies over Germany, was that these aircraft had limited flight endurance. For the Allies, this meant that the fighters, when operating from Britain before D Day, could escort the bombers only as far as Aachen in Germany. Drop tanks were developed to overcome this problem, but they reduced the manoeuvrability of the fighter and proved highly inflammable, despite experimentation with various types. The introduction of the P-51 Mustang, a long range fighter with a speed of over 400 miles an hour, was very important and, in a sense, the end of a line of development, which had

started in the late 1930s with slow twin-engined fighters like the Fw 189.

In this section we examine some of those key fighters of the war.

The Messerschmitt Bf-109

In 1939 Germany had one of the most efficient and best equipped airforces in the world. The combination of Luftwaffe fighters and bombers with the Panzer divisions led to the brilliant Blitzkrieg victories in Poland and western Europe. The mainstay of the German fighter force in the early years of the war was the incomparable Messerschmitt Bf-109 (also typed the Me-109).

The Bf-109 was designed in 1935 by Willy Messerschmitt for the Bayerische Flugzeug-

werke at a time when most fighter pilots were still enthusing over the biplane. The fighter pilots, basing their views on First World War experience of aerial combat, held that the most important characteristics of a fighter plane were manoeuvrability (with emphasis on an extremely short radius of turn) and rate of climb. The monoplane, with its higher wing loading, would not turn as sharply as the biplane, though it more than made up for this by speed, rate of climb and sturdiness.

Messerschmitt believed in the monoplane as the design of the future. Without any experience in fighter design, Messerschmitt entered a competition for a new monoplane fighter with the leading biplane fighter manufacturers, Heinkel, Arado and Focke-Wulf. Messerschmitt worked on the principle of joining the most powerful engine available to the lightest and cleanest airframe that it could take. In his design he utilized all the latest technological innovations, from stressed-skin metal frame to Handley Page slots. At the test trials at Travemunde, the Bf-109VI flew circles around its competitors. Powered by a Kestrel V engine of 695 horse-power, is attained a maximum speed of 292 miles an hour at an altitude of 13,000 feet with a maximum ceiling of 26,300 feet. By 1939, the Bf-109's amazing performance in international competitions created a legend.

The first production model of the Bf-109 was the Bf-109B-1 powered by the Jumo 210D engine of 635 horse-power, giving a maximum speed of

Below: The Me-109, a fighter with a reputation

Above: German Stukas in formation. Below: A Spitfire banks sharply

292 miles an hour at 13,100 feet and a top ceiling of 26,575 feet. Armament consisted of three MG 17 machine guns.

One point in which Messerschmitt had not modernised his plane was the wooden fixed pitch propeller. Complaints led to the installation of the Hamilton-Standard two-bladed variable pitch prop which vastly increased performance. Note how important it was for a modern fighter to utilize all the latest technological inventions in order not to fall behind in the race for power. A poor climb rate was deadly in the face of enemy attack (the variable pitch prop always provided a better rate of climb than the old style propellers), for height was one of the chief advantages in a dog fight, enabling the attacker to dive on his opponent out of the sun.

The Bf-109B-2 was an up-engined version of

Close formation flying by two Hurricanes of the R.A.F.

the B-1 and it was used to great advantage by the Kondor Legion in the Spanish Civil War.

Prelude to War

The Bf-109 was the first fighter plane to incorporate the revolutionary breakthroughs of the inter-war years; it became, in the words of Adolph Galland, German ace and Luftwaffe Inspector-General of Fighters, 'at the time (1935–1941) the best fighter plane in the world.' In its first battle test the Bf-109 proved beyond a shadow of a doubt that a new age in aerial warfare had arrived.

The Spanish Civil War (1936–1939) was a prelude to the greater war to come. It was on the battlefields and in the skies over Spain that the Germans and Italians tested out their new weapons of war. The Germans especially were eager to test out the might of their rejuvenated war machine.

By 1937, it was a well-known 'secret' that the Germans had sent the Kondor Legion, under General Sperrle, to fight with Franco. The German pilots were, initially, flying the Heinkel 51 biplanes, but ran into unexpected difficulties against the Soviet-built I-15 and I-16 fighters. The call went out for the Bf-109. In the spring, the first two squadrons of *Jagdgruppe 88* were equipped with the Bf-109. In July, 1937, the surprise appearance of the Bf-109s turned a major Republican offensive at the Battle of Brunette into a costly stalemate which the Republicans could not afford. One Republican pilot wrote after the event: 'We lost one hundred and four Republican airplanes and approximately twenty-five thousand men. The Nationalists of Franco lost only twenty-three aircraft and about ten thousand men.' The balance of power had shifted dramatically.

The fighter pilots had inherited from the First World War fighter tactics based on the capabilities of their old style machines. The development of the modern fighter necessitated a change of tactics. From the close formation adopted at the end of the First World War the German pilots evolved a loose 'finger-four' pattern, fighters grouped in pairs with a lead fighter and a wingman. The responsibility of the wingman was to protect the leader from a rear attack, his vulnerable point. Two pairs formed the finger-four (so called because it resembled the layout on the human hand).

As was pointed out earlier, it is the combination of superior weapons and proper tactics that make for a victorious war machine. The Germans had both. The combination of the finger-four and the Bf-109 made the Luftwaffe the supreme aerial fighting machine in Europe for two years.

By 1945, some 33,000 of the Bf-109 series were built – more than any other fighter in the war. But, by 1940, advanced Allied designs were creating machines that could more than match the Bf-109. Some of the first to debunk the myth of the Bf-109's invincibility were the British Supermarine Spitfire and the Hurricane, the two fighters that helped to win the Battle of Britain.

The Spitfire

The Spitfire had its origins in the Schneider Trophy races – the most prestigious aeronautic meeting in the twenties. R. J. Mitchell, chief designer for the Supermarine Aviation Works, was determined to build a craft that would sweep the races. In doing so he laid the foundations for the future fighter.

The prototype Spitfire, serial number K5054, began to take shape in 1935. It was built around the powerful new Rolls-Royce Merlin engine (bore – 5·4 inches, 6-inch stroke, and 27-litre capacity). The Spitfire Mk I achieved a take-off power of 880 horse-power and a maximum of 1,030 horse-power. It climbed to 20,000 feet in 9·5 minutes, and reached a maximum speed of 362 miles an hour at 18,500 feet. It had a ceiling of almost 32,000 feet. Combat range was 400 miles. The Spitfire was armed with eight ·303 inch Browning machine guns mounted in the wings. Later models replaced some of the machine guns

with 20 mm Hispano cannon. The test on March 5, 1936, surpassed all existing British specifications for fighter aircraft. As a result, in June of that year, the first production orders for the Spitfire were issued.

Like all modern fighters, the Spitfire was a cantilever monoplane with stressed-skin wings and a monocoque fuselage. The two-bladed wooden propeller of the prototype was soon replaced by a three blade, two pitch, de Havilland prop. Later still combat experience showed that the German Bf-109 had the edge in rate of climb. This was due to its VDM three blade, constant speed airscrew. The Spitfires were converted to a similar system.

The Spitfire was a wonderful machine, received enthusiastically by R.A.F. pilots, who revelled in its light, sensitive touch. In 1939 there were 400 Spitfires in service, ready to combat the German menace.

The Battle of Britain

In July, 1940, Hitler drew up plans for an invasion of Britain, code-named, 'Operation Sea Lion'. The first step in the proposed invasion was a command to Goering, Commander in Chief of the

The four-bladed propellers of these later Spitfires provided even better performance

Luftwaffe, 'to overcome the British air force with all means at its disposal and as soon as possible'. Goering, bloated with pride in his air force, misled by intelligence reports, and under-estimating the strength of his rivals, predicted that the British would be brought to their knees within a matter of days. That his boast did not come true was due above all to his stupidity in transferring Luftwaffe attacks from R.A.F. bases to civilian centres of population. It was also due to the morale of the English people, the radar installations set up prior to the war, and the pilots of the R.A.F. flying Hurricanes and Spitfires.

As long as the Luftwaffe concentrated on R.A.F. airfields and aircraft factories they were on a winning track. British losses were high; German ones comparatively low. In August the R.A.F. lost 338 Hurricanes and Spitfires in combat and 104 badly damaged; the Germans lost 177 Bf-109s and 24 badly damaged. Hitler, however, kept pressing Goering for a quick and victorious end to the air operations in order that Operation Sea Lion, the invasion of Britain, could get under way. A harried Goering decided that a change of tactics was called for. He directed the Luftwaffe bombers to attack London and other major population centres. This was to be his undoing, for the shift in targets enabled the R.A.F. to recoup its losses and thus hold a strong defensive line against the German raids.

September 15 is remembered annually as Battle of Britain Day, a crucial turning point in the air battle. On that warm Sunday morning in 1940, Mr. and Mrs. Churchill visited the underground operations headquarters of 11 Group. Girl plotters of the W.A.A.F. read out the increasing number of enemy aircraft crossing the Channel. By 11 a.m. there were 250 German bombers and fighters intent on destroying London. Air Marshall Keith Park sent two squadrons of Spitfires to engage the enemy over Kent, followed by three additional squadrons and the remainder of 11 Group. Five squadrons of 12 Group led by Group Captain Douglas Bader joined the fray. A total of 200 British fighters were ready to grapple with the enemy.

The fierce determination of the British to fight for every inch of sky slowed the German advance. The bombers were neither able to mass not to concentrate their bombing. To make matters worse the short-range Bf-109 escort planes had to turn back shortly after arriving over English soil. In the end the Germans were forced to drop their loads wherever they could, scattered over miles of London's southern suburbs, and to beat a hasty retreat. The first wave ended in disaster for the aggressor but the assault was not yet broken.

Two hours later a second stream of German bombers and fighters came storming over the Channel. This time over 300 British fighters were sent aloft to stem the tide. Park committed his total force. There were no reserves to throw in at the eleventh hour. Appraising the situation, Churchill remarked, 'Never has so much been owed by so many to so few.'

It was not long before the two forces engaged in combat, and for 10 minutes the fate of England hung in the balance. Tracers zipped through the air; aircraft, billowing black smoke, plummetted to the ground; others disintegrated in mid-air. A confused mass of aircraft ducked in and out of formation or looped round and round in desperate struggle. Slowly, the German formation began to crumble. The German fighters, running low on fuel, turned, one by one, back to the mainland. Suddenly the storm was over. The sky cleared of enemy aircraft. The back of the assault was broken and London was saved. Operation Sea Lion was postponed indefinitely.

P-51 Mustang

P-47 Thunderbolt

Focke-Wulf 190

THE LONG RANGE FIGHTERS

One of Germany's great blunders in her pre-war planning was the lack of a long range fighter. The absence of a long range fighter escort proved disastrous in the Battle of Britain. With the beginning of the strategic bombing offensive against Germany the British, too, felt the effects of the absence of long range fighters, as did the American air force.

In August, 1943, an American air raid on the Schweinfort ball-bearing factories suffered a 16 per cent casualty rate. A follow-up raid in October suffered a loss of 198 (out of 291) bombers lost or damaged. Faced with increasing casualty rates the Americans halted the raids until a long range escort was put into production.

The P-51 Mustang

Thus was born the P-51 Mustang, one of the most successful planes of the war.

The Mustang was powered by a Packard V-1650-Merlin 1,650 horse-power engine. It had a maximum speed of 440 miles an hour at 30,000 feet, and a maximum range of 2,200 miles with drop tanks. Armament consisted of four 0·5-inch Browning machine guns.

The P-51 was superior to its equivalent German fighters, the Focke-Wulfe 100 and the Bf-109. It could fly faster, dive deeper, and turn tighter. The appearance of the P-51 in the opening months of 1944 ended Germany's last hopes for dominance in the air. By March, 1944, the P-51 had conquered German airspace.

The Mitsubishi Zero

Towards the end of 1943 the Americans had finally developed the potential of long range fighters, fighters that meant death to the Luftwaffe. Yet the long range fighter was not a new idea, for on the other side of the world the Japanese had produced an aircraft which gave them, in the first years of the war, undoubted air superiority over the Pacific – the Mitsubishi Zero.

'Of all the elements,' writes one historian, 'in the vast Japanese war machine that brought to pass that country's astonishing success, no single item was more important than the Zero.'

Until 1935 most of the Japanese aircraft industry was based on European and American designs. At that time, however, it was felt that the Japanese had gained enough experience to go

it alone. A year previously Horikoshi, the designer of the Zero, had been working on a fighter design, the first Japanese monoplane fighter, the A5M Claude. The Claude supplied the navy's air forces and was a decisive factor in Japanese victories over the Chinese during the Sino-Japanese War of 1937. One lesson learned during the war against the Chinese, the same one that the Europeans would learn later, was the necessity of long range fighters to escort bombers on their missions.

So, in 1937, the machinery was set in motion for the production of the Mitsubishi Type OO. The new fighter was powered by a Mitsubishi MK2 Zuisei 13 engine producing 875 horse-power. It was fitted with a Sumitomo-Hamilton constant speed propeller to make full use of the engine's capabilities. To gain speed, weight had to be reduced, and inventive means of construction were brought to bear to make the aeroplane as clean as possible. The wing was constructed of a single piece and a new 'extra-super' duralumin was used for many of the parts that went into

the new plane.

The Zero was designed with one specification – to attack and to destroy. To save even more weight and to increase manoeuvrability, the Japanese pilots forwent the usual protective devices – self-sealing fuel tanks, armour plating, and parachutes. Armament consisted of two 7·7mm machine guns firing through the propeller and two 20mm cannon on the wings.

The Battle of Chungking

The Zeros first saw action in China in the late summer of 1940. They ran escort for bomber missions to Chungking, seat of Chiang Kai Shek's Nationalist government. For three weeks the Zeros and the bombers flew to their target without a challenge. The bombers roared over the city and dropped their payload, daily pounding the buildings into rubble. The Zero pilots were anxious to test their new planes in combat and did all they could to tease their opponents into the air, without success.

Finally, on September 13, after the daily bombing mission had been completed, 13 Zero pilots received word of a number of Chinese pilots preparing to land at their home fields. The Zeros turned about rapidly and began to climb to gain the all important advantage of height. High above the city with the sun behind them they waited. When they pounced on the Chinese, they took the Chinese fighters (flying Soviet-built I-15 biplanes and I-16 monoplanes) completely by surprise. Within a half hour all the Chinese fighters had been shot down. The Japanese suffered no losses.

The pattern for the Zero success story was established. For four long years the Zero dominated the skies over the Pacific. Three years before the P-51, the Zero achieved long distance performance. Without the Zero fighter it is doubtful whether the Japanese advance over the Pacific world could have been so swift and destructive. The Zero was to the Japanese what the Bf-109 was to the Germans, and the Spitfire to the British – a great plane and a great fighter.

A Mitsubishi Navy Type Zero. These planes dominated the Pacific War for four years

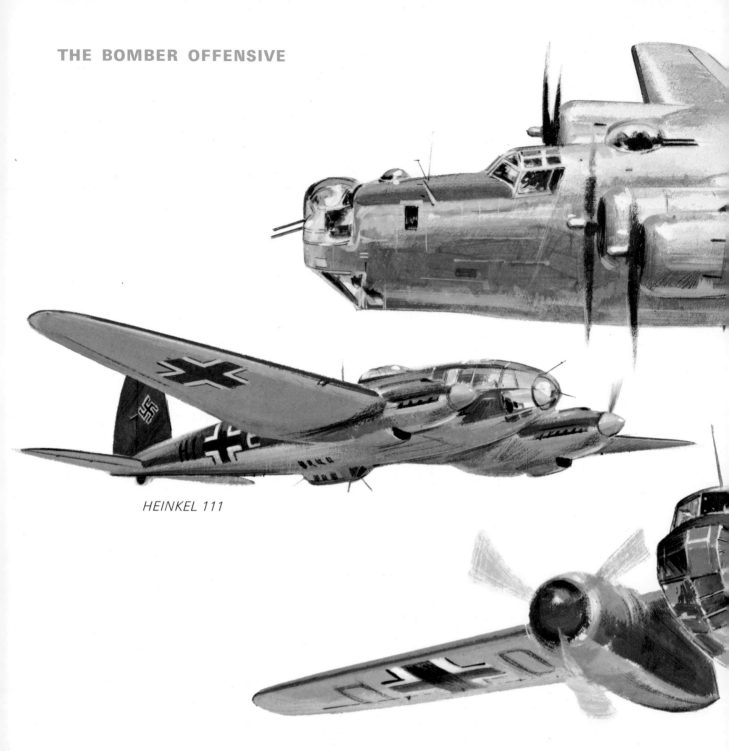

HEINKEL 111

The fighters were the heroes of the air war in their sleek, fast monoplanes, twirling and turning in the sky. It was difficult not to be captivated by their skill and showmanship.

Yet the fighters purpose was secondary, a tactical rather than strategical weapon. Ground attack and escort missions were the stuff of their life. The strategic importance of the aeroplane as a war machine was, it was claimed, to be found in the bomber offensive.

The German bombers were basically designed to support advancing ground forces (the Americans adopted this tactic for the Pacific war). The

Stuka dive bomber is one example of this concept, but the He-111 and Do-217 were also close-support bombers. They were used in a strategic role over Britain, but were not designed for this and proved ineffective.

The British aimed to use their twin-engined Wellingtons, Blenheims, Hampdens etc. in daylight raids. They quickly found that they were too lightly defended and too slow. So the British adopted night-bombing techniques. When the four-engined Lancaster came into service in 1942 it was used in this role, after a few abortive attempts at daylight raids. One drawback with

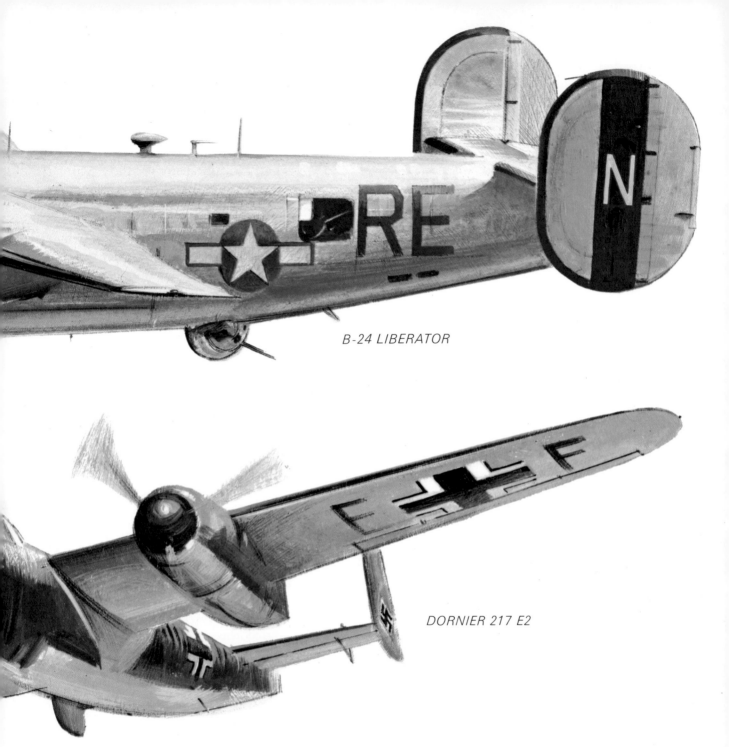

B-24 LIBERATOR

DORNIER 217 E2

the British machines was that their ·303 machine guns were outclassed by the 20mm cannon of the Fw 190s.

The Americans developed the self-defending bombers, such as the B-17, B-24 and B-29. After heavy losses over Germany in 1943 they had to abandon deep penetration raids without fighter escort (and therefore tacitly admit that the self-defending bomber was a myth). They did, however, normally attack during the day.

Another difference between the American and British over Germany was that the British carried out 'area bombing' (i.e. aiming at the centre of towns), whereas the Americans claimed to carry out 'precision bombing' against factories and military targets only. Despite their claims, accuracy in navigation and bomb aiming was a constant problem for both British and American airman, though results improved with the development of radar aids.

The Trumpets of Jericho

Curiously enough, the German dive-bomber force had its origins in a visit by Ernst Udet, First World War ace and Luftwaffe general, to the United States, where he witnessed the performance of some Curtis 'Hell Divers'. Udet was very impressed by their performance, and convinced Goering of their potential. The attraction of the dive-bomber lay in its ability to achieve pin-point accurate bombing without the aid of bombsights, which until well into the war were of very poor quality. Under Goering's prodding the German aircraft industry hastened to produce their own version of dive-bombers. By the spring of 1937 the first Junkers Ju 87A Stukas were on the production lines. A year later, a new and improved model, the Ju 87B was being shipped to Spain.

The Ju 87B-2 had a maximum speed of 238 miles an hour at 13,400 feet, a ceiling of 26,200 feet, and was armed with three 7·9mm machine guns. Its bomb load consisted either of one 1,100-pound bomb or one 550- and four 110-pound bombs. At maximum loading it had a range of 370 miles.

The dive-bomber was a new weapon and it achieved extraordinary successes in Spain and in the early stages of the war. Its victories were due to a combination of accurate bombing and surprise. To the uninitiated, the Stuka, diving out of the sky at enormous speeds and producing a shrill, high-pitched scream ('the trumpets of Jericho'), was a frightening event. The noise produced a kind of panic reaction among ground troops. So, in the early days, the Stuka bombed merrily away without much interference from anti-aircraft fire.

In Spain, during the Civil War, and in the Blitzkrieg, the Ju 87 built up an extraordinary myth of durability and destructive power. But once the initial surprise had been overcome the Stuka proved to be very vulnerable. During the Battle of Britain the Stuka suffered such heavy losses that it had to be withdrawn from the battle. This was because they were not designed for aerial battle. They continued to be used extensively in other theatres of war, especially Russia, as effective *blitzkrieg* weapons. Yet in its day the Stuka had been one of Germany's most powerful war machines.

Blenheim and Wellington

The R.A.F. entered the war with the twin-engined Blenheim. It was an all-metal monoplane with retractable undercarriage powered by two 920-horsepower Bristol Mercury radial engines. Armaments consisted of ·303 machine guns in a dorsal turret and a 1,000-pound bomb

load. It had a maximum speed of 262 miles an hour and a range of 1,800 miles. A Blenheim was the first R.A.F. plane to fly into Germany after war was declared.

It was the Wellington, however, that formed the mainstay of the R.A.F. bombing force until 1941, when the new heavies, the Stirling, Manchester and Halifax, came off the production line.

The Wellington was characterized by an amazing ability to endure a great deal of punishment. The secret lay in the geodetic (lattice-work) construction. The six-man-crew bomber had a range of 1,325 miles and a maximum speed of 255 miles an hour. It was armed with six ·303 Browning machine guns and up to 6,000 pounds of bombs.

The Durable Lancaster

England, in its pursuit of a durable, long range, heavy bomber, finally came up with a winner in the Lancaster. 'By far the most effective heavy bomber which the Royal Air Force despatched on war operations,' in the judgement of Group Captain Leonard Cheshire.

The secret of the Lancaster's success lay in its durability. As Air Chief Marshall Sir Arthur Harris, Commander-in-Chief of Bomber Command, wrote in 1947: 'Its efficiency was incredible, both in performance and in the way in which it could be saddled with ever increasing loads.'

No other British bomber could have survived the pummelling given to the Lancaster, nor could have carried the enormous new, armour penetrating bombs designed by Barnes Wallis.

The Lancaster was designed by Roy Chadwicke for the Avroe Aviation Company. It was developed from the two-engined Avro-Manchester, which had an aerodynamically sound frame, but was underpowered by its Rolls-Royce Vulture engines. By refitting the frame with four reliable Merlin engines the Lancaster was born.

The Lancaster was built of light alloy, and powered by Four Rolls-Royce Merlin XX engines delivering 1,280 horse-power each. Fully loaded it attained a maximum speed of 275 miles an hour at 15,000 feet, with a ceiling of 19,000 feet. It had a maximum range of 2,530 miles decreasing to 1,550 miles with a 22,000 pound load. Its armament consisted of a Frazer-Nash nose turret with two ·303-inch Brownings, a mid-upper turret with two ·303s, a tail turret with four ·303s, and a ventral turret with one ·303. The first production model flew in October, 1941.

Two sturdy British bombers of the early war years. Above: Wellington. Below: Blenheim

Above left: Sir Arthur Harris, who praised the Lancaster. Above right: Waiting in the half light before a raid

Above: Load capacity and toughness were the mark of the Lancaster. Below: A Fortress of Coastal Command

The B-29 Superfortress

If the Lancaster was the queen of the heavy bombers then the B-29 Superfortress was the king, the supreme bomber of the Allied offensive.

In the autumn of 1939 the Kilner-Lindbergh report, commissioned by General Arnold of the Army Air Corps, recommended the development of long range medium and heavy bombers. The outbreak of the European war in September added urgency to the report, and in November the first studies were conducted on the feasibility of a very long range heavy bomber. Thus was born the B-29.

Specifications were sent to four companies for bids. Boeing won. A year later the prototype B-29 was completed. This embodied a number of radical design changes which astonished the aviation world. Faced with the problem of building a bomber of almost twice the weight (98,000 pounds) of the B-17 Flying Fortress, with a 30 per cent increase in speed and only an 80 per cent increase in horse-power, the engineers came up with a revolutionary thin, low drag wing.

Construction methods were improved to make the B-29 an aerodynamically clean aeroplane. Thus, all rivets were flush, and the landing gear folded flat into the wing. Improvements of this

Clean lines helped to give the heavy B-29 Superfortress outstanding range capacity

nature made the bomber a tidy, streamlined, aeroplane.

Another new feature of the B-29 was the pressurized cabin which maintained an atmosphere equivalent to 8,000 feet at an actual altitude of 30,000 feet. The front and rear pressurized portions of the warplane were connected by means of a tube placed over the large bomb bay doors.

The B-29 was powered by four Wright R-3350 engines developing 2,200 horse-power each. It had a maximum speed of 365 miles an hour at 25,000 feet, a cruising speed of 220 miles an hour and a range of 5,830 miles. It was armed with 10–12 ·5-inch machine guns and one 20mm cannon. Bomb load varied between 8,000 and 16,000 pounds.

By the spring of 1944 the Superfortress was ready to enter into action. Based in Chengtu, in eastern China, the 20th Bomber Command launched strikes against Japanese occupied China and the Japanese home islands.

The capture of the Marianas Islands in the summer of 1944 meant that a base could be established for a regular bomber offensive against Japan. The offensive culminated with the dropping of atomic bombs on Hiroshima and Nagasaki.

THE ATOMIC BOMB

On July 16, 1945, President Truman was informed that an atomic bomb had been successfully detonated in the New Mexico desert. The greatest weapon in human history had been created. After much thought Truman decided that the new weapon must be used to bring a hasty end to the war. Orders were given for a squadron of B-29s to be modified to carry the new bomb.

The modifications were limited to the bomb bay, and included a new bomb frame, hoist, sway braces, and release unit. Tests on the modified B-29 had been going on since February, 1944 and were completed by the following August.

In the summer of 1944 a special squadron, the 509th Composite Wing, was formed to drop the bombs. The squadron leader was Colonel Paul W. Tibbets, Jr. For the next few months, until the bomb was ready, the unit spent long hours practising dummy runs, simulating precision bombing, and practising overwater navigation. In July, 1945, the 509th was moved to Tinian, an island in the Marianas group. Last minute testings continued until August 4, two days before the first drop.

The first atomic strike took place on August 6, 1945, in a B-29 commanded by Tibbets. Tibbets had named his craft the *Enola Gay*, in honour of his mother. A little before three in the morning of the 6th Tibbets and his crew assembled on the airfield. The ground crew had already prepared the *Enola Gay* for take-off. The *Enola Gay* carried the 'Little Boy' bomb, as the atomic weapon was called, weighing about 9,000 pounds. The bomb was not assembled until the plane was airborne in case the plane crashed on take-off.

At 9.15 a.m. Tibbets was over Hiroshima. He had not met with any opposition. The release button was triggered, the bomb bay doors opened, and the bomb, with a parachute attached to it, toggled free. Within minutes 78,000 people were dead, another 51,000 injured. The most destructive weapon in recorded history had been unleashed.

A second drop on August 9 – this time on Nagasaki – convinced the Japanese of the futility of further resistance. The Second World War was over, and the B-29 Superfortress had been instrumental in bringing it to its conclusion.

Above: Destruction caused at Hiroshima by the atomic bomb   Below: 'Fatman' nuclear bomb, used on Nagasaki

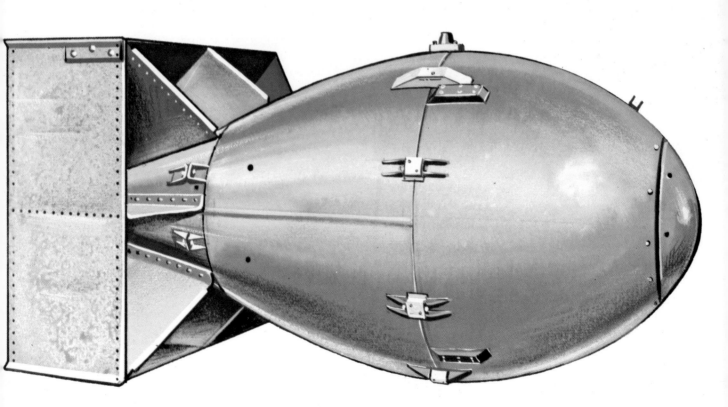

Below: A Grand Slam leaving a Lancaster during the attack on the viaduct at Arnsberg

Above: A 2,000 pound bomb is made ready for loading

ADAPTING THE BOMB

It was not only bombers that were becoming bigger and better as the war progressed, but the load they carried as well. Right to the Second World War bombs remained small and fairly primitive. The growing concern with strategic bombing offensive meant that attention was directed toward the weapons that had to do the job. The end of the war saw an enormous variety of bombs – incendiaries, high explosives, personnel fragmentation bombs, armour piercing bombs, smoke bombs etc. Of these bombs a few stand out for their ingenuity, size or deadliness.

Tallboy and Grandslam

In 1941, Dr. Barnes Wallis, controller of Armament Research at Vickers-Armstrong, began to work on a high capacity armour piercing bomb. He reasoned correctly that the enemy's resources would be moved to underground concrete bunkers, against which the conventional

bomb was useless. Barnes Wallis proposed to combine armour piercing capabilities with a high capacity explosive bomb. The result was Grand Slam, an 11 ton bomb carrying six to seven tons of high explosive in a sleek casing. When released from 40,000 feet the bomb could penetrate 135 feet of sand, exploding subterraneously. But the Grand Slam was too enormous a concept to grasp in the early stages of the war, and a scaled down version, Tallboy, saw action before its parent bomb.

Tallboy was a 6 ton missile, 21·5 feet long and three feet in diameter. One of its most notable successes was the sinking of the *Tirpitz*, Germany's greatest battleship.

Operation Paravane

The *Tirpitz* was the sister ship to the *Bismark*, a massive fortress of 45,000 tons of guns and armour plate. Attempts to destroy her by mini submarines and torpedoes had failed. On November 12, 1944, 38 Lancasters of 617 squadron were despatched on a mission to sink the *Tirpitz*. The great battleship was located at Haak Island, near Tromsö in Norway, just within reach of a Scottish base.

The Lancasters left their base, Lossiemouth, at three in the morning. Six hours later they arrived over the *Tirpitz*. The ship was taken completely by surprise. The big bombers zoomed in on their targets and dropped their lethal load. Twenty-eight Tallboys were dropped, two of them direct hits. The *Tirpitz* could not withstand the assault of the super bombs. She jack-knifed and sank in the shallow waters.

The Dam Buster

Barnes Wallis was a busy man during the war. Aside from aircraft design and the creation of the two largest bombs in the war, he invented one of the most unusual bombs of the war – the skip bomb. The skip bomb was purpose-built to destroy vital German dams in the Ruhr.

The skip bomb was a drum shaped device containing about three tons of high explosive. It was meant to be dropped spinning from a height of 60 feet onto the reservoir. The bomb would then skip to the dam, sink and explode at the base.

The story of the dam buster squadron, the 617,

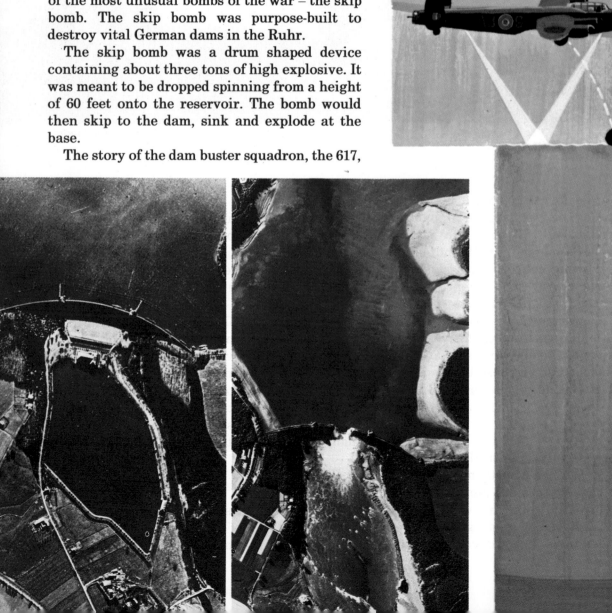

The Barnes Wallis 9,500 lb. bouncing bomb which destroyed the Moehne Dam (seen before and after the attack, below left) was held inside the bomb bay by a special mechanism which caused it to revolve in an anti-clockwise direction. This gave it spinning momentum, making it bounce as it struck the water from a height of 60 feet — pinpointed by search lights fore and aft of the plane which converged when the plane was at the right height. The bomb bounced over the torpedo nets and exploded against the dam wall.

Left: The Moehne Dam before and after

under the leadership of Wing Commander Guy Gibson, is too well known to go into here in detail. Let it suffice to say that, under the most gruelling conditions, the Moehne and Eder Dams were breached causing extensive flooding and costing 1,000 lives. Great though the achievement of Barnes Wallis and squadron 617 was, in the end the Germans were able to repair the damage quite quickly, thus showing the limitations of the aeroplane as a war machine.

Every Kind of Bomb

General purpose high-explosive bombs (HE) made up the majority of the two million odd tons of ordnance dropped during the war. Carried by bombers and dropped in freefall, they varied in weight from 100 to 3,000 pound. About half the weight was explosive charge. The HE's operated on blast effect (a 500 pound bomb would carve a crater 30 feet in diameter and about 15 feet deep,

in an average estimate; the actual impact depended naturally on the nature of the terrain being bombed). To be effective the bombs had to hit the target directly or very close by as even simple shelters provided protection at a 70 yard range.

Fragmentation bombs were similar to the general purpose HE bombs, but carried only 14 per cent by weight of explosive charge. The remainder was taken up by wire wrapping to increase the shrapnel effect. Fragmentation bombs were used in anti-personnel attacks, and on sensitive targets like truck convoys.

Cluster bombs were developed to achieve uniform coverage over a large area (a problem not solved by making the standard bombs larger). Small bomblets were packaged into a single canister. The canister was blown open, usually by compressed gas, just above ground level, spreading the bomblets over a radius of several hundred feet. In later developments of the

Bombs on target, photographed through the bomb bay doors

Above: A viaduct destroyed by Lancasters. Below: The dramatic effect of napalm in the jungle

cluster bomb, 600 bomblets, each holding 2 ounces of explosive and 300 steel pellets, were fitted into a single canister. The fuses on the bomblets could be set to explode on impact or operate on a time-delay mechanism. Targets, as in fragmentation bombs, were personnel or vulnerable equipment.

One of the most vicious incendiary bombs developed was the napalm bomb. Napalm – gasoline jellied by mixing it with soap powder – placed in thin containers was dropped over the target. A central core surrounded by white phosphorous detonated on impact throwing the napalm over distances of 100 feet. The phosphorous ignited spontaneously thus lighting the highly inflammable napalm. Napalm burns with a very hot flame and is very difficult to extinguish. It is a sticky substance and attempts to brush it off only succeed in spreading it.

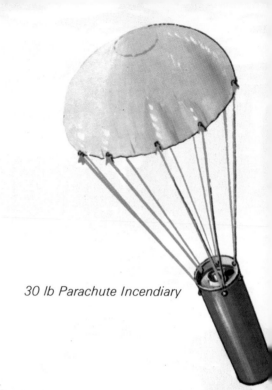

30 lb Parachute Incendiary

12,000 lb HC

12,000 lb 'Tallboy'

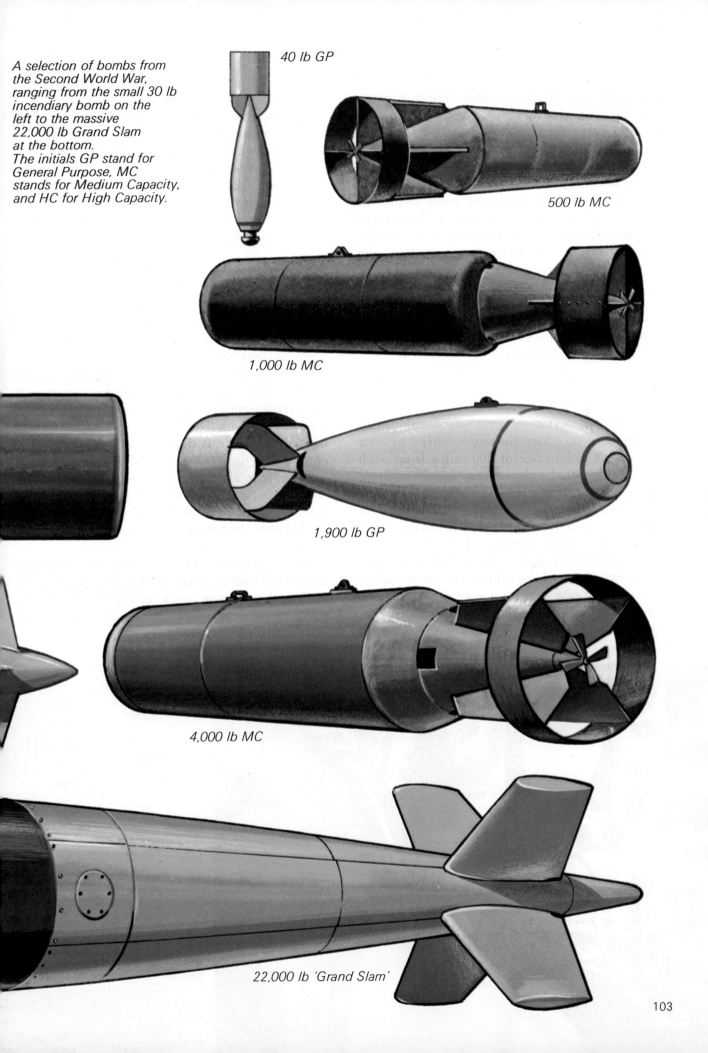

A selection of bombs from the Second World War, ranging from the small 30 lb incendiary bomb on the left to the massive 22,000 lb Grand Slam at the bottom. The initials GP stand for General Purpose, MC stands for Medium Capacity, and HC for High Capacity.

40 lb GP

500 lb MC

1,000 lb MC

1,900 lb GP

4,000 lb MC

22,000 lb 'Grand Slam'

WARNING AND GUIDANCE

In 1936 a research group under Robert Watson-Watts built an experimental radar device, and in so doing opened a new era in air warfare. Not only could radar detect invading aircraft, but it also enabled the British bombers to develop greater accuracy in their bombing missions.

Radar operates by bouncing radio beams off any given object. Receivers pick up the echo of the rebounding beams and relay it to an oscilloscope where a trained radar operative can calculate how far away the unidentified object is.

By 1939 a perimeter of 20 early warning radar ground stations were established in the southeast of England. Without these stations it is likely that the Germans would have been successful in the Battle of Britain.

The Gee System

The Gee system was the first one developed to aid bombers on their missions. Three ground stations, at a distance of 200 miles from each other, transmitted pulses to the bomber. There was one master station and two subsidiary, 'slave' stations. The navigator on board the bomber, measured the time difference in receiving transmissions from the two slave stations relative to the master pulse. He could then plot the Gee co-ordinates of the plane. The co-ordinates were printed as a grid on a special Gee map of Europe. By checking the calculated Gee co-ordinates with the map, the navigator got a fix on the aircraft's position.

The margin of error varied between one half to five miles and effective radius of the Gee system was about 300 miles, enough to take the bombers into the Ruhr valley. Gee's most important contribution was as an aid to dead-reckoning navigation, finding the way into the enemy's territory and getting out again. More helpful as a blind bomb sight was Oboe.

Cat and Mouse

The accuracy of bombing in anything but perfect weather was dismal. One way round the problem was introduced with the Oboe system. Two radar stations, 'cat' and 'mouse', at about 100 miles from each other, transmitted signals to the bomber. The 'cat' station maintained the aircraft on a predetermined course by radioing a series of dash and dot impulses. The aircraft radar showed dots if the aircraft deviated to one side of the course, and dashes if to the other side.

When the aircraft was direct on course the radar emitted a steady beam. The 'mouse' station, meanwhile, signalled the aircraft as it passed over the target. As soon as the signal was received the bombs would be released.

Oboe's principal limitation was lack of range, a mere 275 miles. As the Allies moved eastwards it did not matter so much for the radar stations could be established progressively closer to the main strategic targets.

Below: GEE indicator unit and controls. Below centre: A typical 'Chain Home' Station

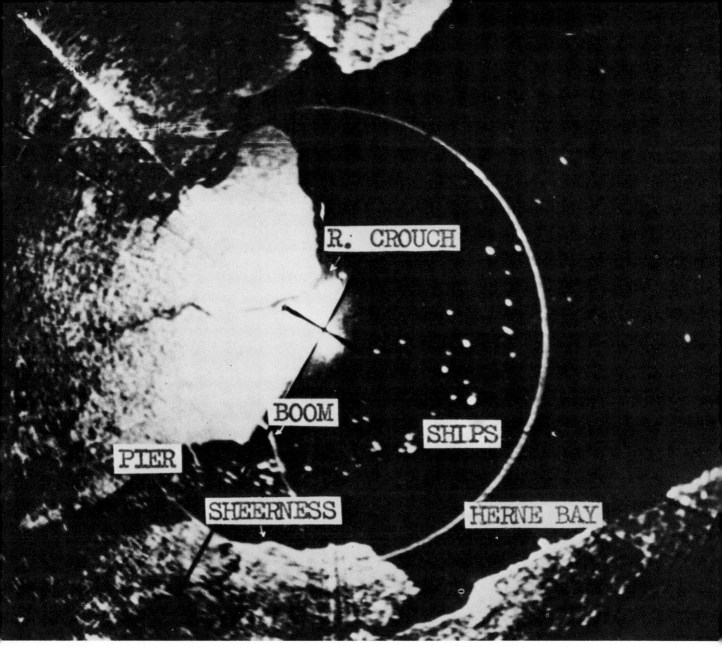

R. CROUCH

BOOM

SHIPS

PIER

SHEERNESS

HERNE BAY

Above: Night radar picture of Thames estuary. Below right: General view of Fighter Direction Station

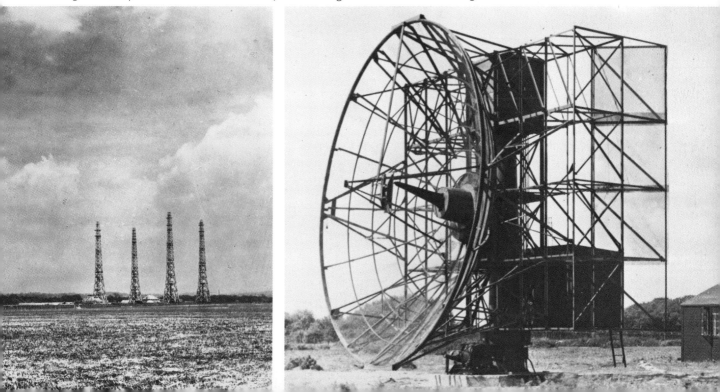

Another limitation was that the home radar stations could only handle a limited number of bombers at any given time. Eventually Oboe found its principal use in Pathfinder Force. The Pathfinder Force was a kind of 'follow the leader' tactic. The lead aircraft, generally a Mosquito, was zeroed in on the target where it dropped a marker bomb or flare. The rest of the bombing force, following closely behind, released their load as they passed over the flare.

Mapping the Route with H2S

H2S was a radar system that did not depend on ground control stations. It used the varying intensity of echoing radar beams to map out the terrain the bomber over-flew. The radar map indicated differences between built up areas and open country, moutains and valleys, the sea and land. The aircraft was equipped with a downward-looking rotating radar transmitter which scanned the countryside, building up a map reading. By comparing H2S readings with known data, the navigator received a pretty accurate fix on the aircraft's position. At the time of the Battle of Berlin more than 90 per cent of Bomber Command was equipped with the H2S device.

A Window for Bombs

One of the most unusual weapons of war ever created were the bundles of long, thin strips of aluminium foil known as 'window'. It is strange that something so seemingly innocuous resulted in the first successful fire-bombing raid of the war.

The reason for the mystery lay in window's ability to confuse German radar. By dropping thousands of bundles of the stuff it blotted out other echoes on the German radar system.

On July 24/25, 1943, a massive Bomber Command force raided Hamburg. That they were able to do so was thanks to the window, which confused German defences. The raid on Hamburg was one of the most destructive of the war causing, over a week, enormous fire-storms which gutted the city and killed 42,000 people.

Oboe system with cat station to direct bomber's path and mouse station to direct bomb on target.

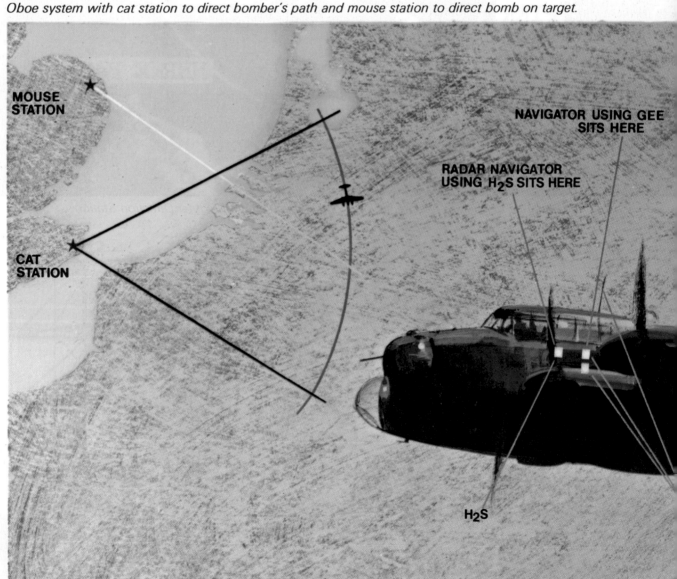

MOUSE STATION

CAT STATION

NAVIGATOR USING GEE SITS HERE

RADAR NAVIGATOR USING H2S SITS HERE

H2S

Above: 'Window' dropped from a Lancaster over Essen, to interfere with radar

H2S

H2S SCANNER

Top: Paul Cornu was the first to take off. Above left: 1925 Autogiro. Above right: Pescara 4S. Below: Fa-61

THE HELICOPTER

In the age of limited wars, that often take the form of guerrilla activity, new types of war machines have been developed or adapted to cope with the situation. Vietnam, in particular, showed the helplessness of traditional types of aircraft in close jungle combat. Airspace was unquestionably controlled by the Americans, but fighters could act as ground support only with difficulty, and the heavy transport planes could not supply troops to the front lines. It was at this point that a slow, ungainly creature took over the functions of the aeroplane. That creature was the helicopter – the latest of the powerful aerial war machines.

The helicopter works on the same principle as the aeroplane. The rotating blades of the rotor act in the same way as an aeroplane wing. At great speeds the airflow will provide the lift necessary to raise the aircraft above ground. The crucial difference, of course, is that the aeroplane as a whole must pick up speed to create the lifting forces on its fixed wings, whereas, in the helicopter, the rotor creates the airflow and thus its own lift. This is the reason why helicopters can rise vertically while aeroplanes cannot.

However, the whirling blades also limit the performance of the helicopter (and it is one of the reasons why it took so much longer to develop than the fixed wing aeroplane). The helicopter suffers from an effect called *dissymmetry of lift*. The term refers to the unequal forces on the rotor blades. The blade passes through a 360 degree circle of rotation. A blade is thus advancing forward against the airflow, or retreating.

The advancing blade naturally has the additional lift of thrust (forward motion), as well as the lift produced by the rotation of the blades. Thus the advancing blade will tend to flap up, and the retreating one down. The flapping effect compensates for dissymetry of lift by changing the angle of advancing and retreating blades.

The retreating blade has a sharper angle of attack, thus increasing its lift, and vice versa for the advancing blade. However, the greater the speed of the helicopter, the greater the flapping effect. Eventually this flapping effect results in serious and dangerous vibrations in the craft. The helicopter's speed is thus limited.

Experiments Take Shape

The principles of rotational flight had been understood for centuries. Experiments had been going on from the earliest days in man's dream of flight, but it was not until the 20th Century that the means were found to fulfil this vision.

Igor Sikorsky at the controls of one of his successful models —the VS-300

The first free flight of a helicopter was made in 1907 by Paul Cornu. His helicopter was powered by a 24 horse-power Antoinette engine, and had two rotors mounted in tandem. The flight lasted about 20 seconds, in which time the craft rose six feet in the air.

Another Frenchman, Louis Breguet, constructed a helicopter powered by a 55 horse-power Renault engine, and supplied with two 25-foot rotors. It rose to a height of 15 feet, and then crashed.

In Russia, a young designer turned his attention to helicopters. Igor Sikorsky's attempts to build a workable rotating wing craft in 1909 ended in failure. Thirty years later Sikorsky returned to his first love and created the prototype of all modern helicopters.

A major step forward was taken in 1924. The Marquis Raul Pateras Pescara designed a helicopter that could move forward, as well as up. Pescara mounted two co-axial rotors on the same mast. Each rotor was on two levels, eight blades per level, 16 blades on a rotor, 32 blades all together – whirling crazily around, driven by a 180 horsepower Hispano-Suiza engine.

Pescara's design enabled the pilot to change the pitch of the blades for added lift (collective pitch control). In addition the craft had a primitive cyclical pitch control whereby the pitch of the blades were changed in cycles creating unequal lifting forces. This allowed the pilot to turn the craft in any direction he wanted.

Despite advances in theory and methods of construction, rotating wing aircraft were still in their infancy by the end of the 1920s. Then a Spaniard, working from a different perspective, created an aircraft from which solved the helicopter's problems.

The Autogiro

Juan de la Cierva was fascinated with the idea of a craft independent of forward motion, and thus less likely to stall. The answer he came up with was an aircraft with free spinning rotor blades – the autogiro. Once an autogiro had obtained some speed the blades would rotate on their own, creating additional lift. If the engine stalled or cut out altogether the free spinning rotors would continue their merry chase round, undisturbed by the lack of an active mechanical motor. Nature takes care of its own, and the airflow from underneath would ensure a gliding descent for the craft.

Top left: Helicopters armed
with machine guns flying
into action in Vietnam.
Centre left: The modern
'cowboy' of the air.
Bottom left: Whirlwind
helicopter of the
Royal Navy.
Above: Sioux helicopters
in formation at a display
in Britain.
Right: Sikorsky HH53
helicopter, armed with
rockets, an impressive
strike weapon

Cierva experimented with various aircraft in the late 1920s, but they all showed a similar fault. Once airborne, the craft evinced dangerous tendencies to roll. It took some time before Cierva hit on the answer and the solution. The problem was dissymmetry of lift. The solution was a flapping hinge to give the blades enough freedom to straighten themselves out. Later a vertical hinge was added to the hub of the rotor. The vertical hinge released massive pressures on the blade root by allowing it to lag, forward or rearward, in the rotor disc. In time these improvements evolved into the *fully articulated hub*, one where the blades are allowed as much freedom of movement as possible.

The military soon became interested in these autogiros. The United States Navy considered using it in an undeclared war in Nicaragua. The still primitive autogiro could not, however, compete with the Marine biplane.

When, in the mid-1930s, the autogiro took off on its first vertical flight (by means of attaching the rotor to a motor while on the ground, and disengaging once airborne), the helicopter engineers stood up and took note. The autogiro had established and proved all the basic elements necessary for creating a practical helicopter. In 1935 the first such helicopter was flown. The honoured man – Louis Breguet.

The Breguet machine was given lift by two rotors mounted one atop the other on the same mast with the drive shaft turning inside another. It was necessary to have the rotors moving in counter directions to offset the torque (turning force) of the motor. The natural tendency of a single rotor machine would be to twist the machine in the opposite direction to the rotor.

The Breguet helicopter featured all the design innovations developed in the previous few years, from articulated hub and cyclic pitch control to collective pitch and differential collective system. In the differential system the collective pitch of just one rotor can be altered, increasing the torque of that rotor. The ship could then turn round on its vertical axis.

Within a year the Breguet was overshadowed by the Focke-Acheglis Fa-61, the finest helicopter design in 1936. The Fa-61 had two rotors mounted on outriggers on either side of the vessel.

The best helicopter of the Second World War was Anton Flettner's 'synchropter'. The synchropter derived its name from the closely inter-

2·75 inch rockets streak forward from a Huey Cobra, capable of firing more than 2,000 pounds of mixed weaponry

meshed and synchronised rotors on the ship.

In 1939, Sikorsky turned his hand to helicopter design and emerged with the VS-300. He revolutionized design by his simplicity. For his helicopter rotors he utilized a penny farthing shape – a large rotor up front and a small anti-torque motor to the rear.

Helicopters developed further after the war, finding their first military use in the Korean conflict, foretaste to come of helicopter service in Vietnam. Helicopters played an enormously important role in the Vietnamese jungle, rescuing sick and wounded, landing troops when and where needed and running reconnaissance missions.

The Huey Cobra

The most effective form of close ground support in guerrilla conditions was found to be the gunship, a natural role for the helicopter. The first helicopter specifically built for that purpose was the Bell AH-1 Huey Cobra.

Its narrow (four foot) fuselage made it a much more difficult target for ground fire, and at a maximum speed of 219 miles an hour it could move quickly away if things got too hot. The AH-1 is powered by a 1,400 horse-power Lycoming T53-L-13 turboshaft engine. Its main rotor diameter is 44 feet, it has a gross weight of nine and a half thousand pounds and a range of 387 miles. But the main feature lay in its armament: a chin turret mounting two 7·62mm six barrel Miniguns and two 40mm grenade launchers; and racks under the stub wings for four rocket packs. The Miniguns can fire at a rate of 1,600 rounds per minute increasing to 4,000 rounds per minute.

The two-man Huey Cobra entered service in Vietnam in 1967 and preparations are under way for a twin-engined version.

CH-54A transport helicopter of the U.S. Army

JET POWER

By the end of the Second World War piston engined aircraft had gone about as far as they could go. Horsepower could not be increased without greatly increasing engine weight and if this could have been done there existed another serious problem – the 'sonic barrier'. As an aeroplane approached the speed of sound the drag increased enormously. Propellers could not cope with that kind of drag and lost all their efficiency. It thus seemed that man was limited to a speed of 400–500 an hour.

In 1928 a young R.A.F. cadet, Frank Whittle, wrote an article for the college paper on the possibility of jet propulsion by means of the gas turbine. The idea was ridiculed at the time, yet in that youthful paper was set the foundation for a profound revolution in aviation.

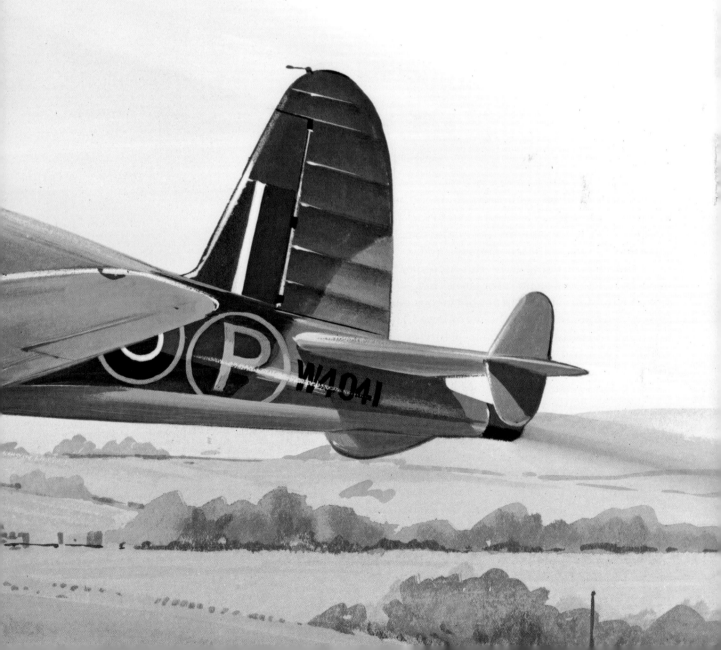

The Gloster E28/39 powered by a Whittle jet. The jet fighter did not come into its own until the last year of the war

Sir Frank Whittle and his successful jet engine

Above: *The Heinke*

Gas turbines had been around since the turn of the century. Many aviators had even thought of adapting the turbine for aeroplane use, but at the time it was still too clumsy, and aviators only thought of using it to run a conventional propeller. There was no interest in that. Whittle asked, why not use the thrust of the hot gases of the gas turbine to propel the aeroplane? The jet, after all, operates on the same principle as the rocket – Newton's Third Law: 'To every action there is an equal and opposite reaction.'

After many trials and tribulations, Whittle managed to have a prototype engine built in 1937, nine years after the idea was first propounded.

The Whittle engine was compounded of three parts. The compressor at the intake end sucked in air and compressed it by means of centrifugal chambers. The middle part was the combustion chamber where the fuel was mixed with the air and ignited. The outlet end contained the gas turbine, a fast-spinning, bladed wheel. A shaft joined the gas turbine and the compressor. The

78, the world's first jet- propelled aeroplane. Below: The Me-262, which Hitler failed to use to best advantage

turbine used the energy of the hot gases to provide useful work. The rest of the hot gases were released through a tiny opening, to increase exit velocity, and, in consequence, thrust.

Four years after the prototype Whittle engine had been built, a Gloster W28/39 took-off from Cranwell airfield – the first British jet.

Although Whittle was the first to propose the idea of the turbojet, the Germans were the first to exploit it. Hans von Ohain had, in the mid-1930s, independently reached similar conclusions as Whittle. But unlike the British pioneer, Ohain did not have to struggle to get a hearing for his ideas. Heinkel, the big aeroplane manufacturer took him in for the express purpose of building a jet aircraft. The result was the Heinkel He 178, the world's first jet aeroplane.

The Menace of the Messerschmitt

Although early development work was being undertaken before the war, the jet fighter did not come into its own until the last year of the conflict. The most important and menacing jet of the Second World War was the Messerschmitt Me 262. It was powered by two Jumo engines developing nearly 2,000 pounds of thrust each. Other radical design features included swept back low wings.

The straight wings of conventional aircraft performed smoothly enough at average propeller speed, but would not do for jets. Experimentation pointed to swept back, thin wings as the solution. The swept back wing provided greater efficiency at higher altitudes and greater speeds, but at a cost – a loss in lift and drag. This meant that jet pilots had to accept a higher take-off and landing speed, and a longer runway.

The Me 262 was intended as a fighter, and as such could have created havoc among Allied Air Forces. With a speed of 525 miles an hour it was at least 75 to 100 miles an hour faster than its nearest rival. Furthermore, armaments consisted of a formidable array of 30mm guns. Happily, Hitler, obsessed with bombing the enemy, ordered the conversion of the whole stock of Me 262s into bombers.

The Turbofan

After the war, jet engined aircraft replaced the conventional armed aeroplanes. In the B-52 Stratofortress, America created the largest bomber and transport jet in existence. The 1961,

B-52 H model had a gross weight of 488,000 pounds with 18,000-pound thrust turbofan engines.

The turbofan engine was thought of in the 1930s, but not developed till much later. The basic idea was the same as the turbojet. Greater power, however, was siphoned off by the gas turbine to drive a large diameter fan at the front of the engine. The fan could be run at a lower spin rate than the turbine by means of a reducing gearing system. The turbofan increased air intake and thrust over the ordinary turbojet, without greatly increasing drag and fuel consumption.

The Soviet answer to the B-52 was the Tu-22 bomber with a thrust of 26,000 to 28,000 pounds and a maximum speed of 1,000 miles an hour.

The Supremacy of the Sabre

Fighters were the aircraft that benefited most

Above: Victor tanker refuelling Lightning in flight. Below: R.A.F. Avro Vulcan bomber

from the jet revolution. Just five years after the end of the Second World War, the United States was at war again. This time the U.S. maintained air supremacy by means of a fleet of F-86 Sabre jets. Swept back wings and a thrust of 3,750 pounds made the Sabre one of the best fighters in Korea.

The Phantom in Vietnam

This jet from the McDonnel-Douglas Corporation, together with the Republic F-105 Thunderchief, formed the workhorse of the Vietnam air war. Powered by two General Electric J79 engines (changed in the British version to Rolls-Royce Spey turbofans) the F-4 reaches a maximum speed of 1,386 miles an hour at 36,000 feet. It has a tactical radius of 550 miles and in addition to a 20mm cannon it can also carry a bomb load of 8 tons.

The Republic F-105 Thunderchief

The F-105 is powered by 26,500-pound Pratt & Whitney afterburning turbojet engine. It has a maximum speed of 1,485 miles an hour at 36,000 feet and a combat radius of 920 miles. Armament consists of a 20mm cannon and a 14,000-pound bomb capacity load. The F-105D were modernized with a new electronic integral bombing system.

Vertical Take Off

One bonus advantage of the invention of jets has been a closer look at Vertical and Short Take-Off and Landing vehicles. The helicopter, though useful, is too slow and cumbersome. It was found that by directing the nozzle of a jet the aircraft could be manoeuvred in the opposite direction. This became the basis of modern research into V/STOL. Turbofans fitted with variable pitch blades can vary the pitch so as to produce a reverse thrust. By adjusting thrust conditions jet aircraft can be made to land vertically and yet maintain their incredibly fast speeds while airborne. The Hawker Siddeley Harrier is at the moment the most famous V/STOL strike fighter in existence. It is, however, still in the initial stages of development. Its full potential is yet to be explored.

MISSILES ON TARGET

The Launching of V-2 rockets towards the end of the Second World War heralded a new era in warfare. The ability of the V-2 to drop on a given target at a speed of 3,500 miles an hour, just minutes after launching, precluding any possibility of interception and defence, was more than impressive. It pointed to the rise of a revolutionary war machine. The subsequent growth in sophistication of rocketry and the addition of sensitive guidance systems ensured that the guided ballistic missile would, if not completely supersede, at least dominate all aspects of war in the future.

Strangely enough, the newest of war machines has a history stretching back hundreds of years to medieval China.

Chinese War Rockets

When or how gunpowder was invented is shrouded in the mists of time. It is known, however, that by the early 11th Century the Chinese were well acquainted with the substance. Soon after, records indicate, gunpowder was being used to propel primitive rocket devices.

The first rockets were of a simple construction – basically metal tubes filled with gunpowder and attached to arrows. But these had in common with the V-2 the basic principle of rocketry, Newton's Third Law of Motion: 'To every action there is an equal and opposite reaction.' In the rocket, the hot gases created by exploding the powder propel the projectile in a direction opposite to the thrust of the gases.

By the 13th Century, batteries of rocket arrows were being built to combat foreign invaders. One of the first recorded instances of the military value of rockets concerns the battle of K'ai Fung-fu in 1232.

The Battle of K'ai Fung-fu

For months the Mongols had besieged the Chinese city of K'ai Fung-fu, just north of the Yellow River. The townsmen had resisted valiantly, but they could certainly not survive another concerted assault by the seasoned Mongol veterans.

Firing a rocket in the early 17th Century

At this point someone must have suggested to the governor of the town that gunpowder might be used to project incendiary rockets against the Mongol horde. Scores of rockets were hurriedly made and fixed into batteries. When the Mongols next attacked, the Chinese were ready and waiting. The fiery (and noisy) rockets were released against the on-rushing enemy, wreaking

Above left: A British naval rocket brigade in 1868. Above right: Rockets firing from HMS Monarch, *1882*

havoc in their flanks. The Mongols feared these fire arrows with their 'thunder that shakes the heavens' more than any other foe. The rockets halted the assault and the city was saved.

The Battle of Seringapatam

The use of the rocket rapidly spread throughout the world, but despite its widespread presence the military value of the rocket went into a decline so that by the 17th Century the main use of the rocket was in fireworks.

The rebirth of the military rocket was inspired, once again, by events in the East. Towards the end of the 18th Century the British fought two campaigns against the ruler of Mysore, Tippoo Sultan. The unusual feature of these engagements was that, in his army, Tippoo Sultan had established a rocketry division of 5,000 men. The Sultan's rockets varied in size, up to 10 inches long and about 2·5 inches in diameter. They had a range of about 1,000 feet. To increase the damage inflicted by the rockets the guiding stick was replaced on some of them by a sword blade three feet in length.

At the Battle of Seringapatam the rockets were no more than of nuisance value (although one English officer wrote of 'the shower of rockets . . . causing death, wounds, and dreadful lacerations.' What Tippoo's rockets did do was focus attention on their military potential. The challenge of designing an effective war rocket was taken up by an Englishman, William Congreve.

The Rockets' Red Glare

Colonel (later Sir) William Congreve was much intrigued by reports of the Indian rockets. His interest in the rockets led to a series of experiments at the Royal Laboratory of Woolwich Arsenal. The result was a 32-pound, incendiary rocket with a range of 2,000 yards. The rocket was an iron cylinder three and a half feet long and four inches in diameter. Clips fitted to the cylinder made it easy to attach the 15-foot guiding stick.

The Congreve rocket got its first trial in the autumn of 1806, during the Napoleonic wars. A British flotilla anchored outside Boulogne, ready to bombard the city. In the space of half an hour, over 2,000 rockets were unleashed on the hapless city. Congreve wrote at the time:

'The dismay and astonishment of the enemy were complete – not a shot was returned – and in less than ten minutes the town was discovered to be on fire.' The following year a fantastic barrage of 25,000 Congreve rockets on Copenhagen caused severe fires and a great deal of destruction.

The Congreve rocket proved itself to be an awesome machine of war. The Europeans hurried to stock their arsenals with this latest weapon. The French, the Italians, the Austrians and even the Russians used them. The British, however, were the rocketeers *par excellence*. They used rockets successfully in numerous campaigns, one of the most famous being the bombardment of Fort McHenry, near Baltimore, in the War of 1812. A young lawyer, Francis Scott Key Parkinson, witnessed the barrage and was inspired to write a verse which told of the 'rockets' red glare'. That verse is now a part of the United States national anthem.

Spinning for Stability

The success of the war rockets led a number of men to seek ways of improving on the Congreve model. An obvious area of improvement was in guidance. Congreve's large guiding sticks were clumsy and inefficient. But what was to replace the stick? A Frenchman, Frezier, experimented with fin-stabilized rockets, but the fins proved little better than the sticks. At about that time rifling was being introduced into artillery to increase range and accuracy. The rifled gun or cannon imparted a spin to the projectile which accounted for the enormous increase in efficiency. Why not do the same for rockets? The trouble was, how could it be done?

An Englishman, William Hale, found the solution. He realized that the exhaust gases of a rocket could be utilized to impart a spin to the rocket. From theory, Hale went on to build the first practical spin-stabilized rocket. He built movable vanes in the tail of the rocket. The exhaust gases forced the vanes to move round

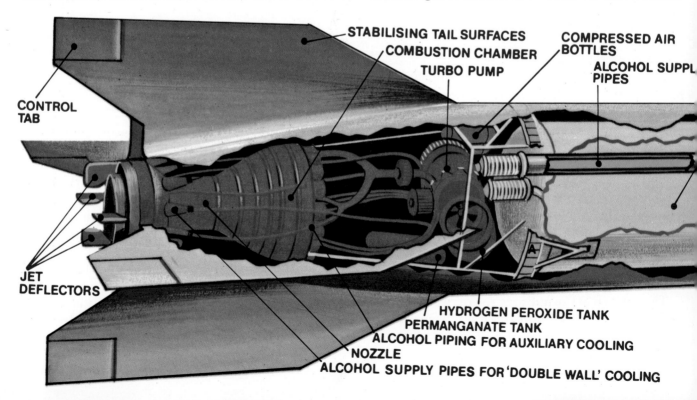

CONTROL TAB

JET DEFLECTORS

STABILISING TAIL SURFACES
COMBUSTION CHAMBER
TURBO PUMP

COMPRESSED AIR BOTTLES
ALCOHOL SUPPL PIPES

HYDROGEN PEROXIDE TANK
PERMANGANATE TANK
ALCOHOL PIPING FOR AUXILIARY COOLING
NOZZLE
ALCOHOL SUPPLY PIPES FOR 'DOUBLE WALL' COOLING

and the vanes in turn spun the rocket.

The Hale rocket replaced Congreve's design and saw action in a number of engagements the most notable of which was the American-Mexican War.

The Mexican War

In 1846, the United States declared war on Mexico. Major General Winfield Scott commanded the U.S. forces. Among the troops shipped to Mexico was a contingent of rocketeers. The rocketeers were sent to besiege the city of Vera Cruz. By the end of March, 1847, the city was surrounded. The American rocketeers bombarded the city with two-and-a-quarter inch six-pound Hale rockets. After five days the city surrendered. The rocket showed that it continued to be an outstanding war machine, but its days were numbered.

The development of improved artillery in the mid-19th Century outclassed rockets in all respects. The decline of the military rocket in the 19th Century was as swift as its rise. But it was not the end of the story of rockets. At the turn of this century, men driven by visions of inter-planetary space travel gave a new lease of life to the rocket.

The Birth of Modern Rocketry

In 1865, Jules Verne wrote a fictional account of a voyage to the moon, *De La Terre A La Lune* ('From the Earth to the Moon'). Little did he realize that his work would inspire the dream of space travel in three men, a Russian, a German and an American – three men who established the science of rocketry as we know it today.

The Russian, Konstantin Eduardovitch Tsiolkovsky, was born in 1857, in the town of Izhevshoye. In 1878, he settled in Borovsk to teach and commence his life's work on the theoretical principle of modern rocketry. In 1883, he made the discovery that would eventually initiate the space age – that reaction flight, as used by rockets, was not dependent on the atmosphere. Tsiolkovsky also postulated that the multi-stage rocket would provide the means of escape from the Earth's gravitational pull.

Tsiolkovsky was concerned with inter-planetary space travel. He would perhaps have been horrified to know that his theories also formed the basis for the latest and most powerful war machines in existence.

The American, Professor Robert H. Goddard, is today acknowledged to be the father of modern rocketry. In addition to a substantial body of theoretical work Goddard initiated experiments with the objective of developing a practical rocket.

On March 16, 1926, Goddard launched the world's first liquid-fuelled rocket. (The fuel was liquid oxygen.) The 10-foot rocket accelerated to 60 miles an hour and flew 184 feet. The first step had been taken. Over the next 15 years Goddard continued his experiments in New Mexico. He worked in comparative isolation from the main-stream of the aviation and scientific world. But

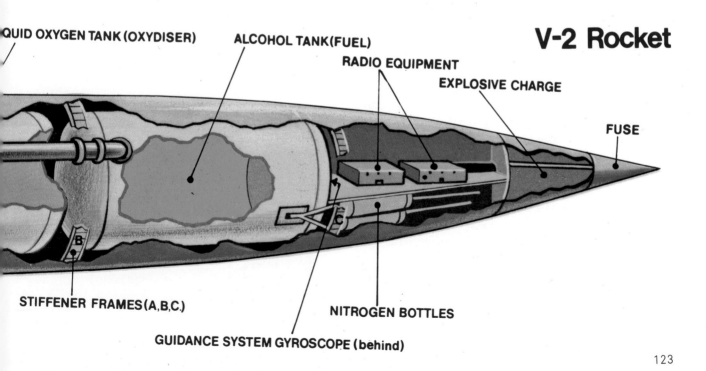

QUID OXYGEN TANK (OXYDISER) ALCOHOL TANK (FUEL) RADIO EQUIPMENT EXPLOSIVE CHARGE FUSE

V-2 Rocket

STIFFENER FRAMES (A,B,C.) GUIDANCE SYSTEM GYROSCOPE (behind) NITROGEN BOTTLES the Second World War renewed interest in the military application of rockets and, by the beginning of 1942, Goddard's group was working on the problems of jet assisted take-off and rocket-propelled missiles.

In Germany, there was a greater public interest in rocketry. Hermann Oberth was a great publicist for the idea of interplanetary space travel and was a prime mover in the establishment of the *Verein für Raumschiffahrt* (Society for Space Travel). His ideas followed along the same lines as Goddard. The VfR formed the basis for Germany's lead in rocket technology during the war.

In the early 1930s the VfR had been experimenting with various rocket engines, with a view to space travel. When Hitler came to power in 1933, the energy of the nation was diverted towards rearmament. No one was excluded from the injunction to make Germany strong. The VfR was disbanded and its chief scientist, Werner von Braun, was attached to the army, with instructions to produce a viable war rocket. In 1937, a rocket base was established at Peenemunde, an isolated peninsula on the Baltic coast. War made the invention of a suitable rocket-launched warhead a matter of urgency. The result was the A-4 liquid propelled rocket, later redesignated V-2 (V for *Vergeltungswaffen*, or revenge weapon).

V-2s on London

Of all the rocket weapons produced during the war, none was more advanced than the V-2. Just under 47 feet long the rocket was made up of four sections. The nose was a conical warhead constructed of quarter-inch thick mild steel and filled with Amatol, a high explosive that could withstand the stresses of a rocket launch. Below the warhead was the instrument section, containing the guidance and control mechanisms. The main body of the rocket was occupied by the two fuel tanks, alcohol on top, liquid oxygen on the bottom. The tail section held the rocket motor, the burning cups, vanes to impart spin, and the *venturi*, the narrow opening in the tail through which the jet of hot gases passed. The principle of the *venturi* was based on the theory that the narrower the opening the stronger the thrust.

For firing, the V-2 was placed on a massive steel ring (the firing table) and below this was placed a blast deflector. After the British bombing raids on Peenemunde in August, 1943, the V-2s were

made mobile by preparing launching sites on railway cars and on trucks.

The rocket motor was ignited by a simple pinwheel device running horizontally inside the motor. The pinwheel, in turn, was ignited electrically by an outside cable which was disconnected just prior to firing. When the pinwheel was lit (by sparks showering through the exhaust nozzle) valves were opened to allow the fuel to flow into the motor under gravitational pull. If the fuel ignited successfully (giving, incidentally, a thrust of seven tons, not enough to lift the 14-ton rocket), the fuel pumps were activated and fed the alcohol and oxygen into the motor under great pressure. The pressure-fed motor produced a thrust of 27 tons, which was then sufficient to launch the rocket on its course. Every second, the rocket lost 260 pounds of weight in fuel consumed. The lighter the rocket

the faster it accelerated, until it reached burn-out stage and began its rapid descent to earth.

The first successful V-2 launch, covering a distance of 119·3 miles, took place at Peenemunde on October 3, 1942. For Werner von Braun it meant the fulfilment of years of effort and struggle and the first concrete step in placing man on the moon. To Hitler and the army generals it meant revenge, a great machine that would reverse the failing fortunes of war. Both von Braun and Hitler were right. The V-2 became the basis for all future space travel, but it also formed the basis for all modern guided missile systems.

By September, 1944, the first V-2s were ready for launching against the enemies of the Reich. The first two missiles were directed at Paris and fired on September 6. They had little success. Two days later the V-2 campaign shifted its focus onto England. From September through to March of the following year about 1,500 V-2s were sent hurtling across the Channel in a last desperate attempt to halt the closing of the noose around Germany's neck. By the end of the campaign over two and a half thousand people had been killed and almost six and a half thousand people seriously injured.

This was a mere dent compared to the effects of the Blitz, yet it did have the effect of causing plans to be drawn up for the evacuation of London – something which had not been done in the Blitz. The V-2 was a great breakthrough in military technology but, like the jet, it came too late to change substantially the course of the war. There was neither time to concentrate the V-2 bombings, nor to refine the rocket's guidance system.

Mobile launcher raising a V-2 into the firing position

A captured Yokosuka MXY-7 Okha

Katyusha, Okha and Bazooka

Though the Germans were undoubtedly in the lead in rocketry, experiments were being conducted in other countries. Three of the most deadly lesser rocket weapons to come out of the war were the Katyusha, the Okha and bazooka.

The Soviets have always been secretive about their military technology. Information about rocketry development is especially hard to come by, but it is known that they had been working on rocket-powered missiles as early as the 1930s. The most famous and the most numerous of the Soviet war rockets was the Katyusha, a solid-propellant infantry support weapon. The Katyusha was six feet long, five inches in diameter and weighed $92\frac{1}{2}$ pounds, of which more than half was payload. The rocket had a range of three miles and was fired from multi-tube batteries, which sprayed a dense barrage on the enemy. The Germans learned to respect the hitting power of the slim Katyusha on their many campaigns on the Eastern Front.

The Japanese effort was less conventional. They used rockets to power their tiny suicide planes in a last ditch effort to halt the advance of the Americans. The most successful of the suicide planes was the Okha, a wooden monoplane 20 feet long and 16 feet in span. The Okha carried a 2,645-pound bomb in its nose and was powered by three 1,200-pound thrust rocket engines, which after a 10 second burn, gave it a speed of 600 miles an hour. In combat the Okha was carried by a parent plane to within 50 miles of the target and, when released, it glided towards its target at a speed of about 235 miles an hour.

On spotting his objective, the pilot then ignited the engine and commenced his rocket-powered dive onto the enemy. A direct hit could sink an aircraft carrier. Though dangerous, there were not enough Okhas to make them a crucial factor in the war.

The Americans had a varied rocket programme during the war, but the best known rocket product was the bazooka, a rocket propelled grenade and the infantryman's friend. The prototype bazooka was seven feet long and 2·36 inches in diameter, although later versions were made more compact to suit combat conditions.

The bazooka was a revolutionary breakthrough in infantry weapons. It made the foot-slogging soldier the equal, under certain conditions, of the heavily armoured tank. It first saw service in North Africa in the autumn of 1942 and soon became standard equipment on all fronts.

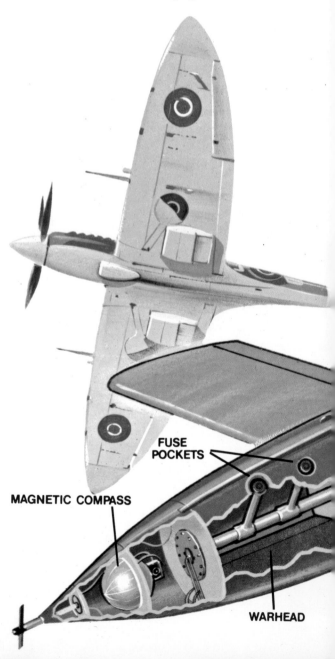

MAGNETIC COMPASS

FUSE POCKETS

WARHEAD

The Guided Missile

After the war the combination of guided missiles, rockets, and nuclear warheads resulted in the most awesome war machine known to man. Experiments with the guided missile had been going on since the early years of this century, but it was not until after the Second World War that guidance systems were joined to ballistic missiles. For years experimenters thought of the guided missiles as a pilotless aircraft.

As early as 1911, American scientists at the Delco and Sperry companies were experimenting with a pilotless biplane called the 'Bug'. The Bug weighed about 600 pounds, half of which was payload, and was powered by a 40 horse-power engine with a gyro-controlled flight direction. When the Bug had flown a predetermined distance a cam was automatically dropped pulling the bolts that attached the wings to the fuselage. The wingless aircraft plummeted, hopefully, on target.

A similar project was undertaken in England. Professor A. M. Low hoped to guide a 'flying bomb' to its target by radio. Development work continued at the Royal Aircraft Establishment at Farnborough, which resulted in monoplanes and biplanes being converted into flying bombs. The two most successful products were the *Queen Bee* and the *Queen Wasp*, both launched by catapult.

But it was the Germans, again, who took the first big step in perfecting a practical guided missile system. In 1942, German scientists began work on a long-range pilotless aircraft, coded Fieseler Fi-103, later redesignated V-1.

The major feature of the V-1 was its pulse-jet engine. The engine fed on gasoline and produced

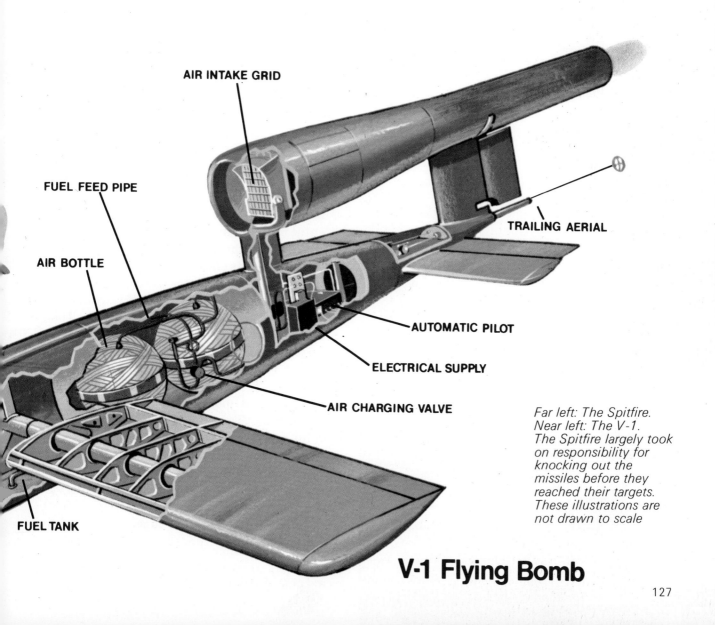

AIR INTAKE GRID

FUEL FEED PIPE

AIR BOTTLE

TRAILING AERIAL

AUTOMATIC PILOT

ELECTRICAL SUPPLY

AIR CHARGING VALVE

FUEL TANK

Far left: The Spitfire. Near left: The V-1. The Spitfire largely took on responsibility for knocking out the missiles before they reached their targets. These illustrations are not drawn to scale

V-1 Flying Bomb

a thrust of 1,000 pounds. The V-1 was 27 feet long with a 17·67-foot wing span and carried about 2,000 pounds of high explosive in its nose. Although the missile was guided by an automatic pilot its trajectory could not be changed once launched. It flew at a speed of 390 miles an hour, a speed which put it at the mercy of enemy fighters and anti-aircraft fire.

Like the V-2, the V-1 was a revolutionary development. Though it made no difference to the outcome of the war it established the trend for future guided missile systems.

From V-2 to Minuteman

The modern military missile is almost completely a product of the United States or the Soviet Union. No other country could possibly afford the great costs that these missile systems entail, although more recently some European countries have begun to develop missile weapons. German scientists captured by the Soviets and the Americans in 1945 established the nucleus of missile development in America and were permitted to take part on the missile development in the Soviet Union. Experiments after the war proceeded directly from where the German scientists had left off, namely the V-2 which provided a basis for further work.

The first successful American intermediate range ballistic missile was the Jupiter. This was simply an improved version of the V-2, but it opened the way for the most fearsome war machines in America's arsenal, the intercontinental ballistic missile (ICBM).

Work on the ICBM began in 1954. Six years later the Atlas showed a range of 9,000 miles. All three stages of the Atlas were ignited before take-off. It was felt that an ICBM would be more efficient if each stage fired separately. The result was the Titan. The Atlas and Titan were both fuelled by liquid oxygen and kerosene, which meant that the fuel could only be loaded just prior to firing. This was a time consuming process and possibly dangerous in wartime conditions. To achieve a faster rate of firing, solid and liquid fuels, that could be stored, had to be developed. An additional advantage of storable fuels was that the ICBMs could be kept in underground, concrete silos, impervious to anything but a direct hit.

Titan 2 was the first missile to use storable fuels. It is more than 100 feet tall and weighs

U.S. Air Force Atlas F ICBM begins a 4,000 mile flight

330,000 pounds. The first stage firing produces a thrust of 430,000 pounds. falling to 100,000 pounds of thrust on the second stage.

The Titan is a heavy, costly machine. The invention of smaller but equally powerful nuclear warheads led to the construction of a solid-propellant missile, the Minuteman – the most successful of the ICBMs.

The Minutemen, as the name implies, are quick-launch missiles, requiring only 32 seconds of pre-launch preparation. The first Minutemen series – LGM-30A – were 53 feet 9 inches long, weighed 60,000 pounds and had a one-megaton nuclear warhead capability with a range of more than 6,000 miles at a maximum speed of Mach 2·2. Guidance was provided by an inertia system.

Improvements led to the development of Minuteman 2 (LGM-30F). This was 59 feet 10 inches long and weighed 70,000 pounds. It had an increased range of approximately 2,000 miles with double the nuclear warhead capacity. Minuteman 2 became operational in 1966 and was destined to replace all previous models.

Multiple Warheads

A major breakthrough in missile systems came with the development of Multiple Independently targetable Re-entry Vehicles (MIRVs). As the name suggests, a MIRV missile possesses several nuclear warheads within one shell, each with its own separate target and guidance system.

The destructive potential of a nuclear warhead in ratio to its size diminishes rapidly beyond a certain point. Thus, a lesser but separate number of atomic blasts is far more effective than one single enormous strike. Since 1969, several Minutemen missiles have been equipped with three 0·2-megaton MIRV warheads.

The Soviet Union has deployed MIRVs in 'Scarp', one of their latest design missiles. This is a two-stage, liquid fuel propelled missile 113 feet 6 inches long with a diameter of 10 feet, which can carry up to three five-megaton MIRVs or a single 25 megaton warhead. It was assumed when Scarp came into operation that 500 of them could effectively destroy the entire United States' ICBM force. Latest research suggests a new factor – the *fratricide effect*. Most of the warheads would destroy one another rather than the target, by radiation from the first warhead, debris, or severe winds which would blow warheads off course.

A Minuteman ICBM on test aims towards a smoke ring

Honest John, a free flight missile, blazes skywards

Safeguard

It was this possibility that led to the development of the 'Safeguard' anti-ballistic missile system (ABM) in the United States.

Safeguard was made possible by recent advances in radar technology, specifically in the development of *phased array radar*. Conventional radar is limited in the amount of traffic it can handle. It uses electromagnetic radiation fed into a single-beam antenna which is mechanically revolved to do its job. In the phased array radar system there is a continuous emission of millions of beams in different directions on a computer-based time phasing. The antenna remains fixed and detection, location and tracking are done electronically, allowing for a greater number of objects to be handled.

In Safeguard, two sets of radar are at work. The *perimeter acquisition radar* (PAR) detects and locates hostile missiles. Once it has fixed position and trajectory of the incoming missile it 'hands over' to *missile site radar* (MSR).

MSR is linked to an intricate computer set-up and not only tracks the hostile missile but also discriminates between warheads and decoys. Once certain of its target it launches the Spartan missile for extra-atmospheric interception, being ready to follow-up with a terminal atmospheric interception by a Sprint missile.

Radar, however, would be practically ineffective in the case of bombardment by *fractional orbital bombs* (FOBS). Under the terms of the 1966 Outer Space Treaty it is illegal to send nuclear warheads into orbit. But anything under one complete orbit does not come within the terms of the treaty. The great advantage of fractional orbit delivery is the element of surprise. An ICBM, with its fixed parabolic trajectory, is a highly visible object. By sending a nuclear warhead into low orbit (approximately 100 miles above the earth) the bomb escapes long range radar detection. The FOB dropped vertically down allows only about three minutes warning. The disadvantages of FOBS are loss in accuracy (no pin-point bombing of missile stations), a reduced payload and a poor ratio of cost-effectiveness.

A Variety of Missiles

The missiles we have mentioned are only a few of those available in the vast and varied collection on the military market today. Rocket and missile technology is an enormous industry quite distinct from general military aviation. Advances are continually being made and the missiles themselves are becoming more and more specialized in their objectives. The range includes surface-to-air, surface-to-surface, surface-to-ship,

American missiles under heavy guard await the orders that will direct their lethal load

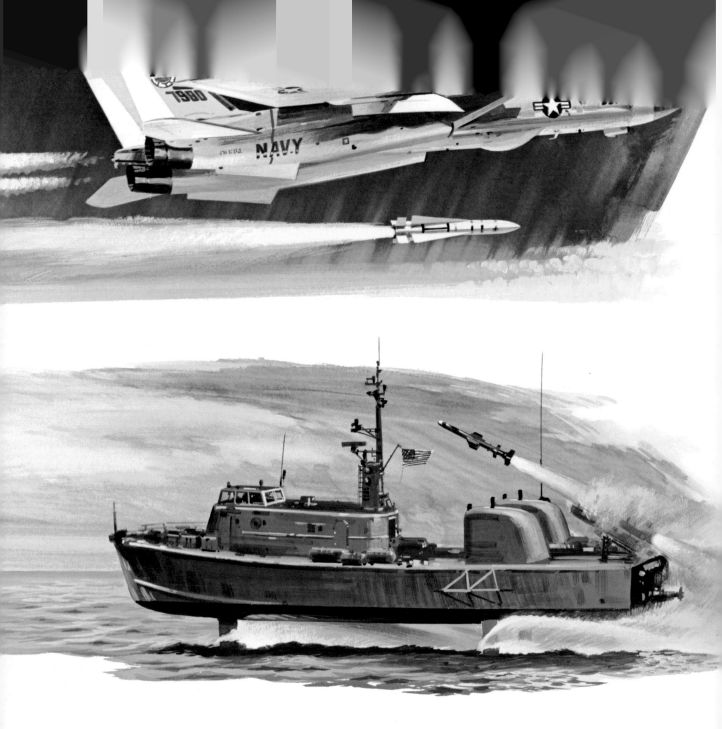

ship-to-surface, ship-to-air, ship-to-underwater, air-to-ship, air-to-air, and air-to-surface missiles.

For instance, there is the interesting and unique Quail which possesses no destructive capabilities, for it is an air launched decoy missile. The reinforced plastic body is stuffed full of electronic devices and stored in the bomb bay of the B-52 Stratofortress. Its stubby wings and fins collapse for easy storage. The Quail is powered by a 2,450-pound engine. Guidance is by automatic pilot. The Quail is 12 feet 10 inches long with a wing span of 5 feet 4 inches and weighs 1,230 pounds. It has a maximum speed of 600 miles an hour and a range of 245 miles. As the parent plane approaches enemy territory the

Top: Hughes AIM-54A Phoenix, long range air-to-air missile, range about 200 km. (125 miles), speed about mach 5+ (4000+ mph). Shown here being fired from a U.S. Navy Grumman F-14A Tomcat fighter, whose AWG-9 computer can control six Phoenix missiles fired at six different targets simultaneously. Above: McDonnell-Douglas AGM-84A Harpoon, anti-ship missile which can be fired from surface ships, sea patrol aircraft or submarines. Range about 60–80 km. (37–50 miles). Can be fired over horizon. Lower right: Manpads (Man-Portable Air Defence System). Designed to replace Redeye missile, which gives the smallest army unit or patrol the ability to defend itself against air attack. Missile homes on target using an infra-red seeker to pick out the 'hottest spot in the sky'—the jet exhaust close to the aircraft's tail

Above left: Soviet SS-13 ICBM (NATO code-name 'Savage') —Intercontinental Ballistic Missile powered by three-stage solid-fuelled booster rocket. Length 20 metres (65·5 feet), range 8,000–10,500 km. (about 5,000–7,000 miles). Carries multiple nuclear warheads. Steered by inertial guidance system, which corrects its own course automatically, given point of departure and point of target.
Above: Lockheed UGM-73A Poseidon C-3 — submarine-launched ICBM replacing the famous Polaris missile in three-quarters of the U.S. Navy's 616-class FBM (Fleet Ballistic Missile) nuclear submarines. Each submarine carries 16 missiles, each reported to carry 10–14 individual warheads. Maximum range 2,500 nautical miles.

Quail is released and acts as a powerful confusing and jamming force. Without it, bombing operations would be almost impossible, for the B-52 could not penetrate the enemy's radar screen.

This particular electronic counter measure (ECM) is just one of many developed in the past few years in a new area of warfare tagged 'the electronic battlefield'.

Senator Barry Goldwater, in United States Senate hearings on the electronic battlefield (Nov. 1970), said: 'I personally think it (i.e. electronic warfare) has the possibility of being one of the greatest steps forward in warfare since the invention of gunpowder.'

The Shape of War to Come

Perhaps we should conclude our review of aerial war machines by taking a brief look at the shape of any future warfare. Like rocketry and guided missiles, electronic warfare is a vast industry which cuts right across army, navy and air force subdivisions. Let us look at a few devices used by the United States Air Force in the war in Vietnam.

In order to fight you must find the enemy, which is not as simple as it sounds given the conditions of guerrilla warfare. Thus, one of the primary functions of electronics is in enemy detection, what is known as *sensor aided combat* (SAC). SAC is a surveillance system which consists of detection devices (sensors) which pick up movements of vehicles or troops; a communications link (usually radio) from the sensor to a 'readout' device. The information is then processed by computer and appropriate instructions relayed to strike aircraft.

The USAF operation of the system, code name IGLOO WHITE, in South East Asia (working out to Laos) was entirely air supported. Sensors were air delivered and the information relayed to aircraft which was then processed in a computer ground station, although some aircraft have processing capabilities. Among some of the sensors used were (a) ACOUSID (acoustic and seismic intrusion detection), (b) COMMIKE (commandable microphone) and (c) ADSID (air delivered seismic intrusion detector).

ADSID, for instance, is dropped and implanted into the ground to the depth of its breastplate, which stops it disappearing completely under the surface, leaving only a camouflaged antenna. Further specifications remain classified.

ACOUSID, 48 inches long with a 3-inch dia-

A detail from Ferranti's laser ranger

meter and weighing 37 pounds, contains only seismic detection logic; that is, it can pick up the tremors of vehicles or personnel. But it can also transmit audio information by means of a small, remotely controlled microphone at the base of the antenna.

According to the testimony of the generals before the United States investigating committee, the sensor devices have been invaluable in detecting and thus leading to the destruction of enemy forces.

Electronics warfare has also affected munitions development, such as in the guided bomb, in which a small TV camera transmits pictures of the terrain to a display unit in the cockpit. The aircrew locks the bomb on the desired target then homes in on the picture onto which it has been locked.

Also in use is a laser guided 2,000-lb. all-purpose bomb. Specifications remain classified but this does point to the future of war machines in the age of limited war.

Progress on remote controlled aerial vehicles and further development in the electronics field point to a state of war where the machines will fight it out while personnel become redundant. Undoubtedly, as in industry, complete automation is the ultimate development.

Above: The QUAIL was a useful decoy missile. Below: The Ferranti laser target marker

INDEX

ACKNOWLEDGEMENTS

The publishers would like to thank the
following organizations and individuals for
their kind permission to reproduce the
pictures in this book:

Associated Press
37, 41

Camera Press
50/51, 58/59, 70/71, 78 (top left),
110 (top and centre)

Expression
2/3, 6/7, 142/143

Mary Evans Picture Library
14/15, 17 (bottom right), 18 (bottom), 19,
22 (top left), 34, 35 (top left), 35 (bottom
right), 36 (top left), 47 (bottom right)

Ferranti
136, 137 (bottom)

Flight International
72, 73

Anne Horton
32

Imperial War Museum, London
62/63, 90 (top left and top right), 90/91,
96, 98, 104, 104/105, 105 (top and bottom
right), 107

Jane's Weapon Systems
137 (top)

Keystone
95 (top)

Mansell Collection
12, 13, 16, 40, 44, 45, 48, 52/53 (top), 53

Popperfoto
8 (top right), 60 (top left), 64, 118/119,
119

John Rigby
54/55 (bottom), 91 (top)

Ronan Picture Library
17 (top right), 18 (top), 20 (centre left),
20/21, 24/25, 26, 28, 29, 33, 35 (top
right), 36 (bottom), 50 (top left), 120,
121 (left and right)

John Taylor
8 (bottom right), 54 (centre left and top
right), 56 (top and centre left), 56/57 (top),
60 (bottom), 61, 64/65, 65, 68/69, 76/77,
80/81, 84/85, 89 (top and bottom), 92/93,
94, 96/97, 100, 101 (top and bottom),
108 (centre left, centre right and bottom),
109, 112/113, 113, 116/117 (top and
bottom), 124/125, 126, 128, 129, 132/133

Spectrum Colour Library
front cover, back cover and 130/131, 78
(bottom left), 78/79, 110 (bottom), 111
(top and bottom)

Artists
Wilf Hardy, Bill Robertshaw, John Young